Environmental Assessment and Management for Exploitation of Minerals in the Area

ISA TECHNICAL STUDY: No. 16

ISA TECHNICAL STUDY SERIES

Technical Study No. 1	Global Non-Living Resources on the Extended Continental Shelf: Prospects at the year 2000
Technical Study No. 2	Polymetallic Massive Sulphides and Cobalt-Rich Ferromanganese Crusts: Status and Prospects
Technical Study No. 3	Biodiversity, Species Ranges and Gene Flow in the Abyssal Pacific Nodule Province: Predicting and Managing the Impacts of Deep Seabed Mining
Technical Study No. 4	Issues associated with the Implementation of Article 82 of the United Nations Convention on the Law of the Sea
Technical Study No. 5	Non-Living Resources of the Continental Shelf Beyond 200 Nautical Miles: Speculations on the Implementation of Article 82 of the United Nations Convention on the Law of the Sea
Technical Study No. 6	A Geological Model of Polymetallic Nodule Deposits in the Clarion-Clipperton Fracture Zone
Technical Study No. 7	Marine Benthic Nematode Molecular Protocol Handbook (Nematode Barcoding)
Technical Study No. 8	Fauna of Cobalt-Rich Ferromanganese Crust Seamounts
Technical Study No. 9	Environmental Management of Deep-Sea Chemosynthetic Ecosystems: Justification of and Considerations for a Spatially-Based Approach
Technical Study No. 10	Environmental Management Needs for Exploration and Exploitation of Deep Sea Minerals
Technical Study No. 11	Towards the Development of a Regulatory Framework for Polymetallic Nodule Exploitation in the Area.
Technical Study No. 12	Implementation of Article 82 of the United Nations Convention on the Law of the Sea Technical Study No. 13 Deep Sea Macrofauna of the Clarion-Clipperton Zone:
Technical Study No. 14	Submarine Cables and Deep Seabed Mining
Technical Study No. 15	A Study of Key terms in Article 82 of the United Nations Convention on the Law of the Sea

Environmental Assessment and Management for Exploitation of Minerals in the Area

Report of an International Workshop convened by the Griffith University Law School in collaboration with the International Seabed Authority in Queensland, Australia
23-26 May 2016

ISA Technical Study No: 16

International Seabed Authority
Kingston, Jamaica

NATIONAL LIBRARY OF JAMAICA CATALOGUING-IN-PUBLICATION DATA

Environmental assessment and management for the exploitation of
    minerals in the area : report of an International Workshop convened
    by the Griffith University Law School in collaboration with the
    International Seabed Authority in Queensland, Australia, 23-26 May 2016.

    p. : ill. ; cm - (ISA technical study; no. 16)

    ISBN 978-976-8241-46-7 (pbk)
    ISBN 978-976-8241-47-4 (ebk)

    1. Ocean mining – Environmental aspects   2. Environmental monitoring
    3. Ocean mining – Law and legislation   4. Environmental management –
        Law and legislation
    I. International Seabed Authority   II. Series

341.455   dc 23

International Seabed Authority
14-20 Port Royal Street
Kingston, Jamaica
Tel: +1 (876) 922 9105, Fax: +1 (876) 922 0195
Website: http://www.isa.org.jm

Contents

Acronyms and Abbreviations

AM	Adaptive Management
APEI	Areas of Particular Environmental Interest
BAS	Best Available Science
BASE	Best Available Scientific Evidence
BAT	Best Available Technology
CBD	Convention on Biological Diversity
CCAMLR	Commission for the Conservation of Antarctic Marine Living Resources
CCZ	Clarion-Clipperton Zone
CCZ EMP	Clarion-Clipperton Zone environmental management plan
CHM	Common Heritage of Mankind
DSM	Deep Sea Mining
EIA	Environmental Impact Assessment
EIS	Environmental Impact Statement
EMP	Environmental Management Plan
ERA	Environmental Risk Assessment
ESIA	Environmental Social Impact Assessment
FAO	Food and Agriculture Organization
ICJ	International Court of Justice
IRZ	Impact Reference Zones
ISA	International Seabed Authority
ITLOS	International Tribunal for the Law of the Sea
LOS Convention	1982 United Nations Convention on the Law of the Sea
LTC	Legal and Technical Commission
MIDAS	Managing Impacts of Deep Sea Resource Exploitation
NIWA	National Institute of Water and Atmospheric Research
OBIS	Ocean Biographic Information System
PRS	Preservation Reference Zones
REA	Regional Environmental Assessment
REMP	Regional Environmental Management Plan
SEA	Strategic Environmental Assessment
SEMP	Strategic Environmental Management Plan
SER	Strategic Environmental Regulations
SPC	Pacific Community
VME	Virtual Maritime Environment

Foreword

The report of the International Workshop on Environmental Assessment and Management for Exploitation of Minerals in the Area makes an important and timely contribution to the work of the International Seabed Authority as it develops a comprehensive Mining Code for the exploitation of resources in the Area. In particular, the report advances deliberations on complex matters relating to the environmental assessment and management of exploitation activities and provides a number of reference points and recommended actions for consideration by the Authority and stakeholders.

A vital component of the international workshops convened by the Authority is to help advance knowledge and expertise in the administration and management of activities in the Area in an objective and transparent manner. Equally, these workshops help to further cement ties between the Authority and its broad stakeholder base of experts.

The Authority welcomed and appreciated the opportunity to co-host the workshop with the Griffith University Law School. The Authority is also very grateful to the Government of the Commonwealth of Australia for its support in funding this workshop and its overall commitment to the development of an environmentally sound regulatory framework for exploitation activities.

On behalf of the Authority, I would take this opportunity to thank all the participants for their individual contributions to the workshop outcomes.

Michael W. Lodge
Secretary-General
International Seabed Authority

Kingston, February 2017

Introduction

The workshop was co-hosted by the Griffith University Law School and the International Seabed Authority (ISA) and convened on the Gold Coast, Australia from 23 to 26 May 2016. Its objective was to address one of seven priority deliverables – High Level Issue No 4 of the Draft framework, High level Issues and Action Plan, Version II, 15 July 2015 – required for the development of the Regulations on exploitation of deep sea minerals identified by the ISA Council at its session in July 2015 (ISBA/21/C/16 Annex III and ISBA/21/C/21.) The Government of Australia, through a Department of Foreign Affairs and Trade Australian Development Research Award Scheme grant is acknowledged for funding the workshop.

Sixty-three participants, from a wide range of stakeholders (contractors, industry, civil society, academic scientists, academic lawyers, government agencies, intergovernmental organizations and members of the Legal and Technical Commission (LTC), supported by the ISA Secretariat and Griffith University), attended the workshop. Attendees also represented a wide geographic diversity (see **Annex IV**).

The participants noted the timeliness of the workshop in providing an opportunity to support and provide advice to the LTC in time for its deliberations on further development of the regulatory framework at its July 2016 session.

Objectives

The workshop had six principal objectives. These were to:

- Outline the content of key principles required for effective environmental assessment and management and their regulation in the Area;
- Set out the contours of key definitions underpinning environmental assessment (consistency in terminology);
- Provide an incremental contribution to the development of the environmental regulations for the Area;
- Deliver a recommended outline of content for a proposed environmental impact assessment (EIA) process and further develop the ISA environmental impact statement (EIS) template, including new guidelines and evaluation methodology;
- Provide additional contributions, guidance and recommendations to the LTC as may emerge during discussions; and
- Consider options for continuing engagement / development of recommendations etc. How can we best harness all this?

Working Structure

Expert presentations on the first day in plenary set the scene for the discussion of a wide range of complex issues relating to robust environmental assessment and management processes and responses.

On subsequent days, the workshop was convened largely in working groups to discuss regulatory issues, working procedures, and suggest time-bound, concrete actions required. This report presents a summary of the discussions and achievements in plenary and working groups and is followed by recommended actions (urgent, short-term and mid-term actions).

Day 1: 23 May 2016

Expert presentations on the first day set the scene for the discussion of a wide range of complex issues relating to robust environmental assessment and management processes and responses. These issues were summarized in seven plenary sessions

- assessment and monitoring of environmental impacts;
- application of the precautionary approach;
- regulatory development;
- enforcement and liability;
- experiences on EIAs and environmental management plans (EMPs) from industry and contractors;
- assessment and monitoring of impacts; and
- adaptive management and definitions.

The following views were highlighted during the plenary sessions.

- At this stage the "Environmental regulations" could be stand alone and be developed separately from the "Exploitation regulations" in order to facilitate their formulation (creating and defining building blocks).
- The regulations should focus on polymetallic nodule resources first, although polymetallic sulphides and cobalt-rich ferromanganese crusts should also be considered.
- The regulations will need to address in a comprehensive approach, a broad range of complex legal issues regarding compliance, enforcement and liability.
- Many standards and protocols already existed that can be drawn on to start drafting exploitation regulations, tailoring them to the specific location and nature of deep seabed mineral exploitation in the Area, subject to the special requirements of the 1982 United Nations Convention on the Law of the Sea ("LOS Convention") and there is no need to reinvent the wheel.
- The importance of geographic, temporal, and spatial data gathering at the relevant scales was stressed when creating impact assessment and management plans.
- The requirement for a clearly defined public participation process: who, when and how.
- Robust determination of environmental baselines, thresholds and triggers is essential before an informed and meaningful site-specific environmental assessment can occur that will inform adequate management. The baseline is very important for assessment while the thresholds and triggers are more an issue for the EMP as that gets into what monitoring and mitigation will be acceptable.
- Adaptive management is a tool that could be applicable in good deep sea mining (DSM) practice where it is judged to be appropriate for the resource in question; it is not an end or a substitute for precaution. It is compatible with the precautionary approach. It requires a certain level of knowledge and ability to impose changes on operating conditions.
- A concern was expressed over a fragmented discussion developing on DSM regulatory development and a need for a more coordinated approach.

On subsequent days, the workshop was convened in working group sessions to discuss regulatory issues, with recommendations on suggested time-bound action required by the ISA and stakeholders. This report presents a summary of the discussions and achievements in plenary and working groups and is followed by recommended actions (urgent, short-term and mid-term actions).

Day 2: 24 May 2016

WG1: Definitions and principles

The first session of the day consisted of a broad-ranging plenary discussion on definitions and general principles that would underpin the application of the environmental provisions of the exploitation regulations. The purpose of this session was to ensure certainty and consistency in the application of key terms. It aimed to define content for later drafting. There was consensus that the International Seabed Authority (ISA) should develop working definitions. However, it was emphasized that the substance of the regulations, and their effective operational context, should drive the definitions and not the other way around. For this reason, it was agreed that the workshop efforts on definitions was a starting point and these would need further consideration as work on the substantive content of the regulations unfolded.

The plenary session benefitted from definitions contained in the Managing Impacts of Deep Sea Resource Exploitation (MIDAS) draft working register of key environmental management terms. Some of these definitions were used as a starting point for discussions. It was noted that there were also well-established definitions in other multilateral conventions and domestic legal instruments that should be considered and drawn on where appropriate and contextualized for exploitation.

The facilitator of the plenary session invited a group of individuals to form a small Working Group on Definitions to continue to work on definitions on the margins of the workshop. **Annex I** of this report contains the efforts of the Working Group. It should be noted that several working groups, such as Strategic Environmental Assessment (SEA) and Regional Environmental Management Plans (REMPs), addressed definitional items directly and these are dealt with separately.

The workshop noted that some general principles should be considered for inclusion in a possible working structure for the environmental regulations, including: best available scientific evidence; an ecosystem-based approach; promotion of access to environmental information including sharing of information and public participation; precautionary approach; best environmental practice; and environmental assessment. It was further noted that additional principles may emerge as development of the regulations proceeded. The workshop considered the first four of these general principles in working groups with a view to providing guidance and thoughts to the LTC.

WG2-1: Working Group on Best Available Scientific Evidence (BASE)

It was agreed that the best available scientific evidence (BASE)[1] should form the basis of an application for exploitation. Best available scientific evidence is derived from employing the highest internationally recognized scientific practices, standards, technologies, and methodologies. Changes occur over time in sampling equipment, techniques, and analysis of data. Hence, best available science (BAS), and BASE are dynamic and evolving processes. However, some science and management objectives are best served by maintaining comparable time series to measure changes over time, or comparability between sites/areas. Hence, BAS may be a combination of maintaining "older historical" approaches and data series, and using new technology.

---

[1] Best available information means the best information that, in the particular circumstances, is available without unreasonable cost, effort, or time. S61 (5) EEZ Act 2012.

It was suggested that to move from the exploration phase to the exploitation application phase, the initial work plan submitted to the LTC for an exploration contract should be part of the exploitation application. A science work programme associated with the initial workplan submitted to the ISA should be detailed, and include sampling design and methodology. Hence BAS can be evaluated from the outset.

There was considerable discussion about the process of review of scientific research being carried out, and its quality. There was consensus that reviews should be conducted on a regular basis to inform the ongoing science plans of a contractor, as well as advising on new research plans.

Best available technology (BAT) was discussed in the context of the use of technological advances in mining operations to maximize mitigation measures. There was general agreement that the use of BAT should be a default position. There was some feeling, however, that different technologies could still be used, as long as the BASE was available to ensure the impacts were within acceptable limits.

An application for exploitation could be considered deficient if the underlying science did not meet the best available standard even if it is the best available. In order to ensure that applications meet the requisite standard, more regular review of the science being done by contractors should be part of the ISA monitoring process. There are currently three occasions when science is reviewed (work plan, pre-test mining EIA, and pre-exploitation EIA) and this may be inadequate if there is a long period between these stages. The ISA has a central role in ensuring that all contractors are using best available science.

WG2-2: Precautionary Approach

In consideration of how to operationalize the precautionary approach, it was noted that there were some best practice models that could be identified on paper, particularly for the Southern Ocean, for instance, those of the Commission for the Conservation of Antarctic Marine Living Resources (CCAMLR), but practical operationalization varied widely. Discussion centred on the need for protective, procedural and institutional measures identified as follows and for which there was broad agreement.

Protective measures: including the commissioning of strategic marine scientific research studies to increase the quality, quantity, and verifiability of the regional environment baseline data and to address fundamental questions needed for effective regional-scale environmental management (this would need funding and action before exploitation begins). Additional measures could include the following:

- The ISA identifying priorities for research to address fundamental questions needed for effective environmental management that would be beyond the responsibility of individual contractors.
- Setting up of a fund to support research and a clearing house to curate the data. Such data should include research done by contractors as well as non-contractor scientific research including existing research results.
- Encouraging Member States to cooperate.

In regard to data handling and management, the ISA should articulate a specific presumption that data is public unless designated confidential.

Procedural mechanisms: including the provision of detailed guidance regarding the requirements for environmental impact assessments (EIAs), and ensuring that the ISA retains the power to amend environmental requirements placed on contractors once a contract is in force. In addition, it was indicated that requirements should not be too prescriptive to allow for procedural mechanisms based on the latest good practice that could be incorporated in the environmental management plan (EMP). The precautionary approach was embedded in the EMP, as such flexibility should be provided in the EIA requirements.

Institutional mechanisms: including the need to ensure independent review and public accessibility of key documents, with a presumption that environmental information is public and confidential information is time-limited. There was also discussion, but no agreement, on the probable need for an environmental or scientific commission to help review EIAs and oversee environmental management.

There was agreement that it would be important for the ISA to retain authority to amend conditions for mining, and even to suspend or stop it. This requires development of clear and measurable criteria, thresholds and triggers, and the ability to act in the face of deleterious cumulative effects. Sponsoring States would also need to retain supervisory authority. Contractors should be required to review and update mining plans and environmental management plans on a periodic basis, and these plans should be subject to independent peer review and public accessibility. On the other hand, there was a general acceptance that the goal post, based on the precautionary approach, should be determined and fixed to provide certainty at the application stage to allow contractors to provide assurance to investors on the operations and parallel EMP.

WG2-3: Promotion of Access to Environmental Information including Sharing of Information and Public Participation

Access to information and participation in decision-making are linked to providing due process to all stakeholders. The working group recognized the Aarhus Convention on Public Participation, Access to Information, and Access to Justice as the starting point for discussion. Not all ISA Member States are States Parties to the Aarhus Convention and, therefore, caution will need to be taken when looking to Aarhus. However, Principle 10 of the Rio Declaration, which is implemented by the Aarhus Convention, is a universally recognized norm that is directly relevant. With this in mind, it was recognized that the discussion pertained to the first two "pillars" of the Aarhus Convention: 1) access to information; 2) public participation. The third pillar (access to justice) was not discussed.

Principles on access to and sharing of environmental information and data are part of provisions in the LOS Convention for the status of environmental information and data. These are not confidential according to Annex III, Article 14 (2) of the LOS Convention and the ISA Regulations on Prospecting and Exploration (regulation 36 (2) Polymetallic Nodules; regulation 38(2) Polymetallic Sulphides and Cobalt Crusts).

The immediate need to establish guidelines and processes to determine the confidentiality of data especially in the context of an EIA process was acknowledged. Resource details were *a priori* confidential whilst environmental data were non-confidential, but there was a grey zone. Some data on resource distribution are essential to determine the distribution of biodiversity. A number of unanswered, but important, questions were raised. The level of detail required to be submitted? What happens to information about resource distribution when it affects the distribution of biodiversity? Should information on the density of nodules, which affects biodiversity and therefore had to be taken into account by an EIA, be made public? These questions elicited divergent views on circumstances when a resource attribute is highly correlated with a biodiversity attribute, and whether the resource attribute should be made public during the EIA process. It was recalled that the principle of non-discrimination among ISA contractors must apply.

The ISA needed an in-house process to resolve potential conflicts and disputes concerning confidentiality and access to data. Some data may be inaccurate. Data should be validated.

It was observed that the EIA rules had to be developed regarding access to information, bearing in mind what would allow for effective public participation.

Issues relating to the accessing and sharing of data are linked to the development of a database housing those environmental data and information generated by exploration activities. The ISA needed to build capacity to share information already available from exploration.

The Working Group saw this as a critical and immediate need. A clear plan (time-bound and implementable) was required to address data archiving and access. What should the role of the ISA be? Should this be done in cooperation with other international organizations? Should existing structures be used?

Working Group 2-3 also worked on relevant definitions. The term "public" was considered in the context of strategy development to achieve meaningful public participation. It was recognized that 'public' had to be defined more broadly than in the restricted context of participation by observers in meetings of the Assembly. For example, in other external ISA meetings, workshops and expert consultations, 'public' is more inclusive. ISA Members also have rights. These are legally distinct from 'public', but should be recognized in the context of EIAs and access to information. Although public input has been limited to data, it could dramatically increase. A broad agreement was reached that access to most information used in the EIA is a basic prerequisite for a meaningful and effective participation. There was agreement that the term 'public' should be interpreted broadly to include contractors, Non-Governmental Organizations, industry, civil society, academia, etc. Formal accreditation should not be a requirement.

Several unanswered, but important, questions were raised. For instance, the procedure for the treatment of public participation comments needs to be clear. At a minimum, comments should be clearly captured. Not every comment had to be addressed, but comments could be grouped by themes. How would public/stakeholder inputs (written and verbal) be considered? If an input was viewed as irrelevant, this had to be noted with a rationale. Some information in an EIA can be treated as confidential. Two principles were referred to; common heritage of mankind (CHM) vs rights of the public affected. The former suggests broad inclusion. Would some stakeholders and bodies have access to greater levels of engagement than the general public? If so, how would this be determined?

Meaningful public participation was dependent on the development of a strategy by the ISA to engage all stakeholders. While the draft ISA communication strategy considered by the LTC at its February 2016 session was recognized, an urgent need for an ISA strategy on multi- stakeholder and wider public engagement and participation remained.

Further discussion was required on public participation and right to appeal. It was not considered further by the working group because access to justice was not discussed.

WG2–4: Ecosystem Approach

An ecosystem-based approach to DSM concerns the protection and preservation of ecosystem functions and services (derived from maintaining key structural and functional elements of communities), and the assessment of proposed DSM activities to ensure there would be no harmful effects on ecosystems on a broader scale. It was emphasized that different ecosystems required tailored approaches. Questions were raised about ecosystem limits. There was consensus that ecosystem-based approaches would vary with the marine environment and proposed type of DSM activity. Identification and establishment of appropriately sized mitigation and conservation areas were recognized as important elements in moving forward. There was consensus that developing the regulatory framework required consideration/assessment of DSM impacts/effects on ecosystem services and functions (including food chains).

The most fundamental prerequisite to the implementation of an ecosystem-based approach is the collection of adequate baseline information. This information can be used by the ISA to prepare area/regional specific ecosystem-based plans which can set out the information contractors are required to collect to make ecosystem-based assessments when preparing applications to undertake exploitation. This baseline information must address aspects of ecosystem function (species relationships and ecological setting, not just ecosystem structure). To date data collection, reporting and sharing have been less than optimal. The ISA needed to set protection/preservation objectives/obligations for regions or areas within which contractors would operate (including the collection of baseline data and ongoing monitoring). Contractors should be required to provide data collected in compliance with those objectives/obligations to inform the development of an ecosystem management plan(s). Ecosystem-based planning should be used to provide contractors with more certainty as to their ecosystem obligations prior to and during exploitation. Contractors needed to demonstrate that their actions will not cause unacceptable harm or be in contravention with the strategic and regional environmental management plan to be developed by the ISA. Contractors needed additional guidance to set priorities for their data collection and studies.

It was agreed that developing the regulatory framework required consideration/assessment of DSM impacts/effects on ecosystem services (or chains of living organisms). The ISA is responsible for developing an ecosystem management approach in order to protect and preserve the marine environment from the harmful effects of deep-sea mining in the Area.

The present Clarion-Clipperton Zone environmental management plan (CCZ EMP) is fit for exploration activities, but there was need to be greater planning to satisfy the ecosystem-based approach prior to exploitation. There would also need to be more cooperation in the exploitation phase between contractors. There was consensus that the CCZ EMP had appropriately retrofitted an area in which licences had already been granted. In the future EMPs should be developed prior to the granting of contracts.

The need to rename Areas of Particular Environmental Interest (APEIs) as 'marine protected areas' was raised, although there was no agreement on this issue.

WG3: Strategic Environment Assessment and Strategic (Regional) Environment Plans

The concepts of Strategic Environment Assessment (SEA) and Strategic Environment Plans (SEMP) to the mineral resources of the Area are conceptually different from those applied in domestic legal systems. Ordinarily, SEA generally applies to government plans, policies, and programs across a wide array of macro areas of regulation (eg energy, transport, freshwater, agriculture, waste).

In the context of the mineral resources of the Area, it appeared as if the ISA's concern was with DSM as the principal, if not exclusive, focal point for strategic assessment. This does not mean, however, that an SEA is carried out with blinders on. The SEA must include assessment of the broader potential impacts and synergies that DSM raises. In carrying out an SEA, the ISA must include fisheries, shipping etc. The view of the working group and plenary was that a 'special' or 'hybrid' type of SEA and SEMP was required. The SEA should provide the general context of seabed mining (including the positioning of seabed mining versus other alternatives and the assessment of competing uses), but should also assist the contractor with its EIA by providing information on possible cumulative effects of global warming, ocean acidification and fisheries. The SEMP is a broad policy plan that addresses environmental assessment issues. It is more of a programmatic assessment. Both the SEA and SEMP should be drafted by the ISA to provide a framework for contractors in the next two to three years.

The SEA and SEMP should provide the framework within which to evaluate contractor EIAs for individual mine sites and to establish EMPs for such sites. This would serve as a mechanism for assessing potential and actual cumulative impacts at appropriate bioregional scales, not only those related to seabed mining activities but also impacts of the combined activities from other marine uses. The SEA and SEMP must be science based and developed by the ISA independently of individual contractors' EIAs, although they should be able to draw on the EIAs and baseline information collected by contractors and other available information in a region.

A SEMP should include provisions for periodic public review, as has been agreed for the CCZ EMP. This is especially appropriate as new information is generated from contractors' accumulation of baseline data, EIAs and EMPs as well as independent research and surveys, and the SEMP should be revised accordingly. Such a review process would also provide an important tool to address cumulative effects of multiple exploration and exploitation activities in a region, as well as to take into consideration cumulative impacts from other activities (and changes such as ocean warming and acidification) affecting the region.

Environmental Assessment and Management

The working groups carefully considered environmental assessment and management issues. These are reported on below as follows: (i) Regional Environmental Management Planning (REMP) Working Group; and (ii) Strategic Environmental Management Planning (SEMP) Working Group. In addition, working groups were held on the environmental assessment and management process that will be required in the exploitation regulations.

Participants expressed a range of views on the development and use of regional and strategic environmental planning. These are demonstrated in the Working Group summary reports.

The following is an attempt by the Co-Chairs to provide clarity and simplicity that is appropriate to the exploration for and exploitation of mineral resources in the Area.

Strategic Environmental Planning and Management is the responsibility of the ISA. It addresses the range of environmental issues associated with the plans, policies, and work programmes of the ISA required to deliver on its mandate and working in collaboration with others with mandates in marine space. There is only one of these.

Regional Environmental Planning and Management is the responsibility of the ISA. It addresses the range of environmental issues associated with different resource types and their location (spatial context) for the protection and preservation of the marine environment. There is a need for several of these regional documents:

    a. Clarion-Clipperton Zone (CCZ) for nodule resources.
    b. Northwest Pacific for cobalt-rich ferromanganese crusts.
    c. Indian Ocean for polymetallic nodules.
    d. Mid-Indian Ocean Ridge for polymetallic sulphides.
    e. Mid-Atlantic Ocean Ridge for polymetallic sulphides.

These regional planning documents are urgently needed. Completion of the review of the CCZ plan is also urgent. The cost of the SEA and SEMP could be borne by States Parties through the ISA budget. It should be in place before the commencement of the EIA process by a contractor (estimated 2-3 years' time). SEA should be drafted for each region (Pacific, Indian, Atlantic Oceans) and each type of deposit. The working group focused on the CCZ.

The environmental impact assessments, statements, and management plans required in the exploitation regulations are the responsibility of the contractor as part of the application process. These documents are required to demonstrate compliance with the relevant regional plan and the ISA strategic plan while also addressing the many issues described in the EIA template and guidelines.

WG4: Regional Environment Management Assessment and Plans

In many respects, a regional environmental management plan (REMP) derived from a regional environment assessment (REA) is an umbrella agreement between different stakeholders overseen by the ISA. The REA reflects a regional framework in which to place contractor activities and obligations, including those related to collaborative marine scientific research, the sharing of data, and mutual support for the minimization of impacts both direct and indirect. While it is an important item in the toolbox, it is only one of the tools for designing a sound EMP. REMPs must consider the potential impacts in the marine environment caused by events activities such as climate change, fisheries, shipping, etc. in addition to mining, and including cumulative effects. These large-scale cumulative effects (global warming, ocean acidification and fisheries) should be assessed under the REA. A periodic update of the REA (e.g. 5/10 years) would be justified. The update may also be channeled through an updated REMP.

The ISA needs to establish, with urgency, a regional environmental assessment process and REMPs with input from contractors, the scientific community and other stakeholders. Contractors, scientists and regional organizations are likely to provide important data on other users and potential conflicts between users in the area. The Secretariat should produce a document detailing the elements to be included in a generic REA and REMP based on the consultation and advice from an expert group. It was recommended that these be reviewed and updated every five years.

It was suggested that a fund be established to finance preparation of regional environmental assessments and management plans, and related activities of the ISA. Whilst this fund should ultimately be capitalized with revenue derived from seabed mining, it was recognized that States Parties may need to provide funds in advance of mining if regional assessments and management plans are to be prepared in a timely basis prior to exploitation.

The ISA needed to consider how to address potential conflicts or interference that may arise from the conduct of scientific research in contractor areas to overcome confusion about rights for scientific institutions. Greater discussion is required on whether it would be useful to determine scientific research guidelines.

The ISA should develop a method to allow scientific expeditions to plan cruises with the cooperation of any activities being conducted by contractors.

REAs and REMPs must be established as early as possible during the exploration phase recognizing that data generated by contractors would be important in REA and REMP decision- making. (There is an immediate need given the number of exploration contracts).

The establishment of those APEIs that would not be mined is a fundamental element of REMPs. Areas protected from mining are necessary, but may not be sufficient, by themselves, in creating an REMP that satisfied the ISA's mandate to protect the marine environment and prevent significant adverse impact from mining.

An EMP should include local, smaller scale areas within contractor areas based on geomorphology. Vulnerable marine ecosystems should be identified and made provision for.

Spatial planning methods must consider genetic connectivity of populations. Biogeographic zones and finer scale gradients evident in satellite observations of primary productivity, including seasonal and inter-annual variability, should be included. Predictive habitat models may assist in planning in areas where there are few data, and planning should include temporal and spatial elements.

The ISA should create an expert group in two to three years to decide on elements of a generic EMP based on the update of the CCZ EMP review and new REMP for the Mid-Atlantic Ridge, Mid-Indian Ocean and nodule areas, and the Northwest Pacific cobalt crust areas to be proposed.

A method is needed for independent scientific research to address the management of the ISA. This includes gathering data from APEIs to determine whether they conserve biodiversity affected in the mining areas and replicate ecosystem-function characteristics.

It was recommended that the ISA support the development of a global fund for advancing cooperation in marine scientific research and capacity building and transfer of marine technology. This was discussed at the second session of the Preparatory Committee established by the UNGA Resolution 69/292 "Development of an international legally binding instrument under the LOS Convention on the Conservation and sustainable use of marine biological diversity of areas beyond national jurisdiction", in August 2016.

It was observed that the legal status of REMPs needed to be clarified in the mining code. In particular, the code should make it clear that the preparation of regional environmental assessments and management plans must be developed and approved prior to issuance of exploitation contracts and that they should be reviewed and revised periodically to ensure they remained accurate and effective in light of new information and practice.

It was not clear if contractors had obligations for the maintenance of regional biodiversity. In other words, should contractors be required to collect data from areas beyond their individual mining blocks?

ISA does not have competences regarding activities beyond mining. However, ISA must recognize other relevant uses of the ocean while exercising its competences (Article 147 paragraphs 1 and 3 of the LOS Convention).

For both SEA/SEMP and REA/REMP, it was suggested that they be developed in parallel as an over-arching Strategic Environmental Regulation to be included in the Mining Code to guide both Exploration and Exploitation regulations. It was urged that it be developed in parallel with the Exploitation Regulations. It was seen as urgent because of general agreement that EIAs for exploitation contracts could not be prepared until an applicable SEMP and REMP was in place. The need for the clear definition of the two concepts was emphasized.

Strategic Environment Assessment/Plan (SEAs) and Strategic Environment Management Plans (SEMPs) Working Group

The Working Group suggested the following elements be included in a SEA/SEMP: reference to existing relevant regulations; information needs of stakeholders; alternative actions (including no-action); cumulative and synergistic impacts (for example ocean acidification, global warming, fisheries, multiple mining operations); technology evaluation; and gathering of baseline data (including that available from pioneer contractors); protected areas. The use of spatial mapping and planning techniques including spatial databases was considered important.

It was recommended that the delivery of the SEA and SEMP be in two parts. The first part would look at existing regulation and information needs, and involve an evaluation of the alternative options for seabed mining. The report would examine the mineral markets and determine the place/opportunity for seabed mining, taking into consideration cumulative impacts and the required technology. This exercise could be outsourced. The second part would involve gathering environmental baseline information collected by contractor(s).

It was noted that the ISA needed to build its capacity to assess the data submitted by contractors. This data would inform marine spatial planning and lead to establishment and optimization of preservation zones within the CCZ. This might lead to the inception of the Mining Inspectorate.

The development of the SEA and SEMP may benefit from BBNJ, the Convention on Biological Diversity (CBD), the SEA Directive of the European Union (EU), MIDAS, the UNDP protocol, and other existing national SEAs, taking into consideration that the ISA SEA is not the "typical" SEA.

The Working Group considered that the SEA/SEMP process would provide input to the contractors on the different cumulative impacts and should be delivered as soon as possible. Once implemented and used as a source of information and general task descriptions, it must be monitored and subjected to regular review, including for compliance. The SEA/SEMP could contribute to a precautionary approach by setting up protected areas and preservation areas, including those needed to: identify uncertainties; establish thresholds which must be low, considering cumulative impacts; and develop the legal regulatory framework.

The Working Group agreed that the SEA/SEMP process should include a discussion on alternative actions/options, for example on plume management, and best practices. It should include a monitoring/compliance with EIA to form a holistic approach. It will be a source of information for the contractors regarding effects from outside the mining blocks.

The Working Group agreed the SEA/SEMP process should be broad (all of environment impacts) in scope, consider overarching issues, and set up the guidance for EIAs and REMPs.

Furthermore, institutional participation should be part of the drafting of the SEA, whilst public participation in the form of a multi-stakeholder process would take place once the report was finalized.

Day 3: 25 May 2016

WG5: Risk assessment

Where there is limited understanding of the environment, it is challenging to assess environmental risk; it was, however, important that it take place. The environmental risk assessment (ERA) process is standard and can be applied to the DSM context. It is important, however, that an ERA strategy be developed for dealing with the high uncertainty related to DSM, and translate this into protective strategies (precautionary/management/mitigation).

There was agreement that environmental objectives, baseline data, ERA, EIA, and thresholds needed to be interlinked. Focused baseline data collection in the context of ERA and EIA was crucial and required before decision-making, and the ISA should keep environmental objectives and meaningful data collection in mind on a routine and ongoing basis.

The WG noted that ERA was dynamic and iterative and widely applicable. ERA ought to be included in strategic assessments and plans and in the entire EIA process, including scoping, preparing environmental impact statements, and management plans. There should, or may need to be, several ERAs conducted through the development of the EIA to EMPs, increasing in the level of quantification. ERA should be undertaken and paid for at regional/strategic level by the ISA and at the project level by the Contractor.

It was felt that periodic and independent review plus stakeholder engagement in the ERA process was needed for transparency. Transparency, accountability, and the need to engage public confidence, were all parts of the process within which the ISA regulates DSM in the Area on behalf of humankind.

Dealing with uncertainty: knowledge gaps existed (baseline data – including biodiversity, ecology, ecosystem function and impact – affect relationships, definition of technology and its effect on environment and ecosystem-based science). Knowledge sharing would benefit the ERA process.

The ERA process should develop an evidence strategy and gap analysis for the ISA, which could then devote resources to resolving uncertainty (e.g., resources from the Seabed Sustainability Fund). Science has to quantify as much as possible the level of uncertainty and suggest whether uncertainty can be decreased through science or if management has to react to uncertainty (i.e. risk assessment versus risk management).

Several other observations made in the working group bear emphasis:
- Uncertainty and scale – not all projects are the same in scale. Note also a step-wise function between pilot mining and commercial mining in uncertainty that needs to be managed.
- Who needs ERA: contractors, equipment suppliers, regulatory authorities, consultants, technical experts and third parties, insurance companies, investors, lenders, Non-Governmental Organizations, and other stakeholders.
- Consistency across ERA approach could (should?) be imposed by ISA in exploitation regulations.
- ERA should be a self-contained document, though it is part of the EIA; i.e., integrated into EIA document (consensus view). Alternative view: separate document.

WG6: Serious harm to the marine environment

There was consensus in the Working Group that the difference, if any, between 'significant adverse impacts', 'significant adverse change' and other definitions used in contemporary instruments should be considered, aligned and built on, and gaps filled to cover all types of harm articulated in the LOS Convention.

Furthermore, there was consensus that the operationalization of serious harm required explicit conservation objectives as well as indicators, thresholds and trigger levels to enable management decisions. The overall objective is to ensure effective protection of the marine environment and prevent adverse impacts or harmful effects, while acknowledging that an extractive activity will, by definition, cause some harm.

There was a discussion about the appropriateness of the threshold of 'substantial evidence' and there were a number of comments that this was a very high threshold. Some views were expressed that the requirement for substantial evidence was inappropriate in the deep-sea environment as it presupposed the availability of onsite evidence which would not be possible and seriousness of impact and extent of 'substantiality' depended on value of the environment being affected and intensity/longevity of the activity itself. One observation was made that perhaps the discomfort with the threshold of "substantial evidence" was because evidence was being equated with proof, which was difficult to obtain in the deep-sea environment. However, evidence could be used to demonstrate probability as well and, hence, the threshold could apply in those situations. This was not necessarily inappropriate. Therefore, it was important not to confuse evidence with proof and criteria. Criteria are likely to differ in the measures and thresholds between resource types.

It was observed that it was up to the decision-making body (LTC advice to Council?) to decide on sufficiency of evidence based on what they had before them and, if insufficient, they should decide whether the activity should proceed. There was a need to ensure the sufficiency of the information provided to determine what would or would not cause lasting irreversible damage.

There was no consensus on the elements to be considered in determining sufficiency (and the level of uncertainty in information), but these should include, for example, scale of the area, resource(s) to be affected, biological characteristics of the area (including endemism), spatial scope of ecosystem (oceanographic data), habitat disruptions, and possible aspects of rehabilitation. It was critical to have a social view of what could/couldn't be done.

The responsibility to provide evidence on a case by case basis was the applicant's. Triggers and thresholds for ongoing review were needed and should be considered in an EIA. Whilst the EIA may be complete, it may not be sufficient in terms of evidence required.

Other issues raised but not discussed included; (i) the critical need to consider management of cumulative impacts and serious harm and what constraints this may pose on contractors; (ii) the critical need to establish standardized terms/requirements re data acquisition to ensure usability/usefulness in the decision making process and to ensure mechanisms for provision of data to the LTC; and (iii) the need for LTC to establish a permanent working group, scientific commission, or environmental commission to review past, current and future scientific research and to advise on definitions, trigger levels for action/inaction.

It was recommended that existing definitions in the regulations should be revised and aligned in light of original PrepCom definition and extensive international legal developments since adoption of the LOS Convention including the ITLOS Advisory Opinion, UNGA resolutions on VMEs, FAO Deep Sea Guidelines, IOC, Espoo Convention, ICJ Judgments (Pulp Mills, Gabcikovo), and International Law Commission work on transboundary harm.

Requirements in other regimes should be examined to consider definition/threshold of 'substantial evidence'. Detailed criteria for guidance regarding what constitutes 'substantial evidence' include setting out the contours of key definitions underpinning environmental assessment, those adopted by the CBD Guidelines on Marine and Coastal Activities, and the FAO Guidelines on Vulnerable Marine Ecosystems.

The need to develop clear guidelines to ensure the sufficiency of the information provided to determine what would or would not cause lasting irreversible damage was emphasized.

Environmental Impact Assessment (EIA) and Environmental Impact Statement (EIS) Working Group

The objective of the Working Group was to advance contributions and discussions towards the development of a best practice EIA process. The focus was on marine environmental aspects and it was suggested to leave social and cultural aspects for later discussion. During the discussions consensus was reached on all aspects discussed. It was agreed that:

- There is no need to reinvent the wheel. There is extensive literature on EIAs; the ISA is the lead agency with the responsibility to review EIAs. States may have their own requirements and may impose those in addition to ISA requirements.
- Considering the stages: the screening stage was straightforward with well-established input. The scoping stage established how the EIA would unfold. The principal recommendation was that the ISA would require capacity and structural changes for efficient and timely evaluation and processing of EIAs. It was noted that the scoping stage may be an iterative process, or through the appointment of an expert facilitator to help guide the contractor through the scoping stage with ISA, which would help prevent objections during evaluation and expedite the process. This again reinforced the need for capacity and structural changes in the ISA to deal with this kind of iteration-consultation approach in the scoping phase.
- The need for an Inception/Scoping Report was key. The group identified that this process provided the contractor with some level of certainty that the studies they were undertaking will fulfill requirements. It was recognized that stakeholder engagement would be useful at this stage – examples were cited that scoping may lead to the recognition of issues that that would be screened out on technical grounds, but screened-in to respond to citizen/stakeholder concern. It was also recognized that notwithstanding the scoping document, the contractor must not ignore new issues that may arise from baseline data collection, the two both of which needed to be balanced.
- Consensus objectives were conservation, development, and a participatory approach. There is a need for participation and transparency around data, how much should be disclosed; the default position was that the EIA needed to be transparent and the data disclosed. While data disclosure

was agreed, points were made as to the consideration that putting the data out may lead to its misuse, and this implied requirements for information management.

- It was recommended that the LTC could start identifying substantive norms of evaluation, and ways that they are identified. This might be in an illustrative, but not prescriptive, manner.
- External experts should do the review of EIAs and auditing, which would provide public assurance, and independent overview while being accompanied by transparency and public participation.
- Geographic scope/scale: boundaries of contracts are not necessarily boundaries of EIA. Rather, EIA should be conducted on an impact area determined by baseline data and modeled to zero effect. It was recognized that options existed for contractors to apply on the basis of a mining plan that may include a single contract area or multiple contract areas with that decision made by contractors on the basis of a commercial-risk profile. Identified necessary criteria must cover baseline data, best practice; temporal variability, and the need to identify multiple strategies on how habitats are studied.
- Recommendation to be made to the LTC that EIA systems that could be used were in place; existing EIA process flow charts should be used as a starting point.

The capacity and structural changes must be in place within next three to four years and new budgetary obligations to undertake the recommended actions be developed by the Finance Committee. However, scoping and EIA content must be in place with urgency to give contractors a reasonable level of certainty. The processing of scoping documents and EIAs must be timely.

WG7.1 and 7.2: EIA legal and scientific process

The objective of the session was to advance contributions and discussions toward the development of a best practice EIA process for the ISA Regulations on exploitation. The focus was to be on marine environmental aspects and it was suggested to leave cultural and social dimensions for later.

The ISA is the lead agency with the responsibility to review EIAs. States may have their own requirements and may impose those in addition to ISA requirements.

There was consensus on advising that there were EIA systems in place that could be used; existing EIA process flow charts should be used as a starting point (see examples of EIA process flowcharts in **Annex II** Western Australia and other EIA process flowcharts).

Objectives of an EIA include conservation, development, and participatory approach. There was need for participation and transparency around data, how much should be disclosed; the default position was that the EIA needed to be transparent and the data disclosed. Points were made as to the consideration that making the data public may lead to their misuse if the underlying quality is not specified. This has implications for requirements of information management.

Regarding the geographic scope/scale, it was pointed out that boundaries of contracts are not necessarily boundaries for an EIA. Rather, it was recognized that options existed for contractors to apply on the basis of a mining plan that may include a single contract area or multiple contract areas with that decision made by contractors on the basis of the commercial-risk profile. Identified criteria centred on good baseline data, best practice, temporal variability, and the need to identify multiple strategies on how habitats should be studied.

Considering the stages of an EIA process, the screening stage was straightforward, with well- established input. The scoping stage established how the EIA would unfold; the principal consensus recommendation was that the ISA would require capacity and structural changes for efficient and timely evaluation and processing of EIAs. This may be accomplished by several different methods, e.g., through contractors, other outsourcing options, and t could be done remotely. A registry of independent experts could be established.

It was noted that the scoping stage may be an iterative process, or through the appointment of an expert facilitator to help guide the contractor through the scoping stage with ISA, which would help prevent objections during evaluation and expedite the process. This again reinforced the need for capacity and structural changes in the ISA to deal with this kind of iteration-consultation approach in the scoping phase.

The scoping document was seen as key. The scoping process provides the contractors with some level of certainty that what they are undertaking will fulfill requirements. It was also recognized that notwithstanding the scoping document, the contractor must not ignore new issues that may arise from baseline data collection, both of which need to be balanced.

Substantive norms of EIA evaluation, and ways that they are identified are needed. It is advisable that the LTC start identifying what those might be, in an illustrative rather than prescriptive manner, to enable the best assessment of particular characteristics of an area/resource. There was consensus that a review of EIAs and auditing should be done by external experts, providing public assurance of an independent overview. The stage at which this was to be done was not agreed.

WG8: Adaptive Management (AM)

The WG agreed that the ISA should decide if adaptive management was appropriate for deep seabed mining, how it should be provided for in the Regulations and how it should be applied. It should not be prescriptive and be at the discretion of the contractor to be able to fulfill the environmental performance objectives. Key reference reports and case study examples of applications were required for the LTC to assist that decision and potentially build AM into the Guidelines.

There was also agreement that if AM was adopted then the definition of AM might combine that from the MIDAS draft working register of terms mentioned above with the addition of a definition on active and passive AM, including temporal and spatial scale definitions. It was noted that active AM would not be applicable to all circumstances, but passive AM probably would be (as good management). However, an evaluation of whether AM was an appropriate tool was needed as in some circumstances (e.g., low uncertainty/low controllability) it may not be. The ISA is to determine where Active AM may be applicable. It was recognized that AM can play a part in the application of the precautionary principle. It was stated that adaptive management is only appropriate when it reduces uncertainty consistently with the precautionary principle. If agreed to be applicable, then the ISA will need institutional resources, capacity, funding and capability. There was agreement that, if adopted, adaptive management must be reflected in the key decision milestones through the life of a project, from application to decommissioning.

A review cycle needs to be defined for AM (on a local scale this is incorporated into the EMP review) and can include options that require activities to pause/adapt/continue or stop. AM does not imply a scenario of contracts being stopped pending review and then re-issued on a cyclical basis over a 30-year contract term. If AM is applied at a regional scale, then ISA needs to consider AM in respect of multiple operators working in multiple operations at the same time in the same region.

There were divergent views on how to incentivize contractors to modify performance to achieve continual improvement. There were divergent views on the need to focus on outcome limits and avoid setting prescriptions on how to do it. There were also divergent views about whether "grandfathering" or "phasing out" of accepted technologies or methodologies should be provided for and under what circumstances (such as new technologies with better environmental performance).

It was felt that there would be a need to define the "reasonable amendments" for adaptive management changes. The review cycle to be defined for adaptive management can include pause/adapt/continue or stop, and may, if adaptive management is used, imply a scenario of contracts being stopped and re-issued on a cyclical basis over a contract term. If adaptive management was to be applied by the ISA itself at a regional scale, then the ISA needed to consider adaptive management in respect of multiple operators working in multiple operations at the same time in the same region.

There is potential to translate the powers of a regulator in a licensing regime into a contractual regime. The ISA should explore what elements of flexibility can be implemented to assist all stakeholders. The review of contracts should explicitly include consideration of compliance and environmental performance outcomes in order to trigger an adaptive management response.

There was agreement for independent audit/review of monitoring data to inform AM responses and that the ISA needed to focus on the process to amend contracts. This could be part of the SEMP/REMP review that could incorporate the results of AM through monitoring results. In any event, it was agreed that the ISA would need further institutional capacity, resources, funding and capability to address AM.

Day 4: 26 May 2016

WG9: EIA decision-making process

A presentation was made to the working group on the U.S. EIA process. This was considered a good starting point and processes could be adapted to take account of the ISA structure. The following areas were discussed and the general process was agreed upon (as shown in **Annex II**).

The starting point is EIA screening – deciding whether an EIA needs to be done. There is the presumption that a new development will require an EIA, but modifications to existing projects are not so clear. The next phase is developing a robust scoping report. Scoping is crucial. It requires consultation with the ISA as regulator to ensure the right approach and direction is taken. Four major points to be addressed by the scoping report are:

- Actions
- Issues
- Alternatives
- Studies to be done. This is a key element. A list of studies to be performed will drive the work to be performed during the EIA process.
- Public participation during this scoping phase is recommended.

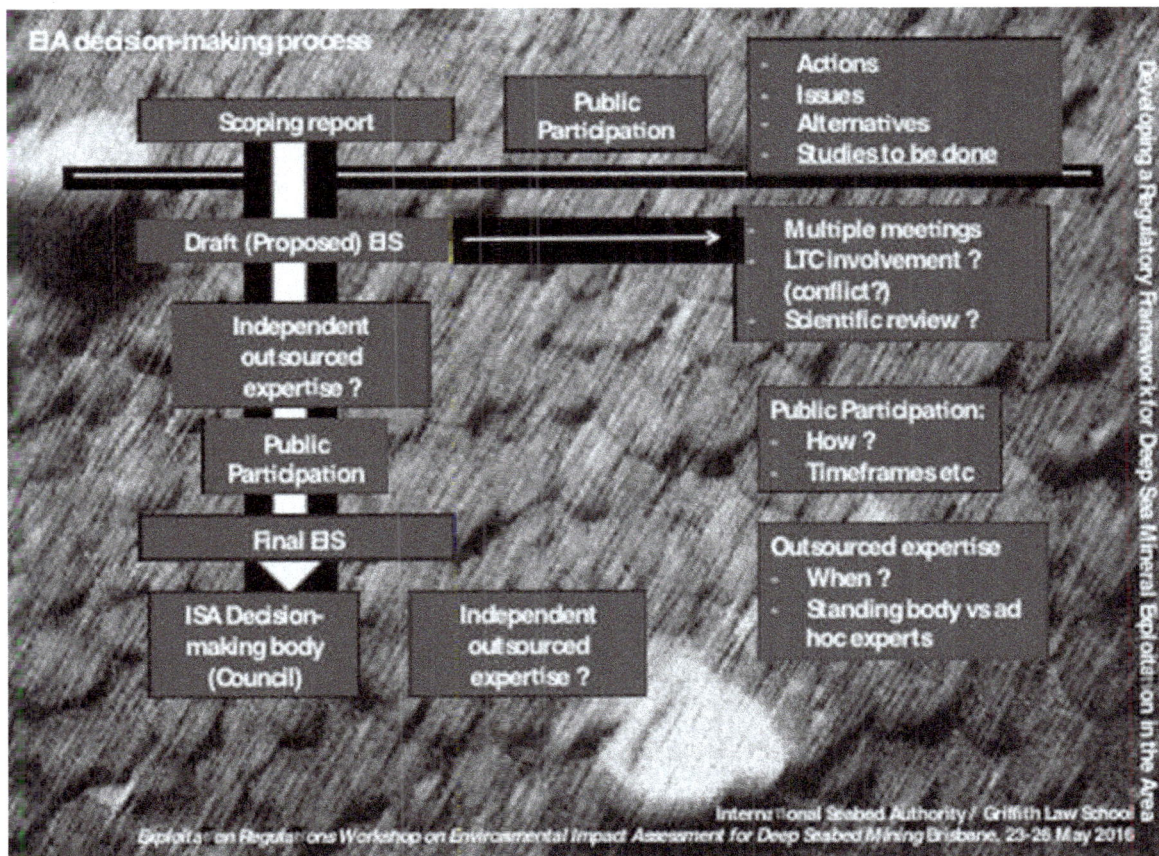

A draft EIA would require multiple meetings with the Secretariat – an iterative process. There might be a need for expert consultants at this stage and a process needed for the engagement of such consultants. Expert (independent) consultant comment could be useful for public consumption but this raised divergent views.

It was considered that the LTC should not be engaged at this stage due to a possible conflict of interest at the later decision-making stage (or any LTC members engaged at this stage should recuse themselves from the later process). It was asked whether a scientific committee should be established at this stage to review the draft EIS.

As to the final EIA, there were divergent views as to the need for any expert review (by tender process?) and/or further public review.

As to the accepting organ or body receiving the final EIA, suggestions included setting up a subsidiary body e.g. scientific body or committee to consider recommendations. The exact nature and status of this standing body or committee of scientific experts was not discussed or made clear. However, concerns were expressed about setting up a subsidiary body versus engaging a group of experts to provide assistance and guidance to the LTC.

Time frames needed to be established for each step of the EIA process. 'Show-stopper' mechanisms needed to be included in the procedure. This was considered crucial for certainty in the process. The role and responsibility of sponsoring States in the decision-making process must be considered, although the risk of regulatory replication needed to be taken into account.

There were points of disagreement on what kind of internal reforms (function rather than structure?) would be needed and on whether this should be the role of the current Article 154 performance review. Any 'major' modification in the final EIS arising from the expert review and the public participation process would trigger a new EIA process with public participation. There would, however, be a need to define what constitutes a "major" modification. This issue of modification was also relevant under any contract issued by the ISA and the need for a fresh EIA process (and public participation). At this stage, the trigger of specific thresholds or criteria relating to performance objectives could be relevant.

As to a public "participation" strategy, the ISA needed to consider/clarify the appropriate use of language: receipt of public comments, review, consultation, participation etc. and the different levels of engagement these terms imply. The LTC should consider "public hearing" / open hearings/closed hearings for the final EIA decision-making and who should be permitted to attend e.g. Observers.

There was a need to consider possible appeal mechanisms in the EIA regulatory process. Consideration should be given to administrative mechanisms as well as dispute resolution under the LOS Convention. Equally, after any final approval, the right of a legal challenge by stakeholders to challenge the regulator's final decision. This question was, potentially, for Member States.

The Regulations should consider the power for the ISA to request further information or commission reports during the EIA process. As to a public "participation" strategy, the ISA needed to consider/clarify the appropriate use of language: receipt of public comments, review, consultation, participation etc. and the different levels of engagement these terms imply. Involvement of sponsoring States in the EIA process needed consideration. The LTC should consider "public hearing"/open meetings for final EIA decision-making and who should be permitted to attend (for example Observers). Some delegates stressed that the linkage between the EIA and the environmental management plan needed to be clear, so that the outcomes of the EIA were reflected in the terms and conditions of the EMP for each contractor's activities. The capacity and functioning of the ISA must be considered. The substance should drive the form: once the decision-making process steps are set, the capacity and functioning can be adapted around it (cf. meeting cycles), not the other way around. This is to be considered urgently. A description of the EIA decision-making process is in **Annex II**.

WG10: EIS Template

The objective and scope was to review the EIS template issued at the ISA 2010 Fiji workshop, as well as others. The National Institute of Water and Atmospheric Research (NIWA) used the Fiji workshop template as a starting point and revised it. The session also looked at NZ EIA legislation, section 39.

It was agreed that the ISA needed to clarify the geographical and jurisdictional extent of the required EIA/EIS, and whether national jurisdiction(s) were included. The ISA also needed to develop a repository of relevant EIA legislation (both international and of member states) for contractors.

It was noted that the ISA should advise contractors on how to identify appropriate stakeholders for consultation purposes (develop contact list). Several points needing clarification were raised: in what language(s) should an EIS report be submitted? Whose obligation was it to provide translations? Produce template in all ISA languages. It was agreed that there should be linkages between EIS to an SEA/REMP and the EMP.

The revision related first to working definitions and understandings. The major outcomes/ revisions of this working group are reflected in work on a template contained in **Annex III**.

WG11: EIS Guidelines

Discussion included a consideration of whether standardization was needed. It was noted that guidelines could deliver a certain ease of evaluation. Alternatively, it raised a possible danger that it might become a box-ticking exercise.

Some viewed the terms EIA and EIS as having the same meaning. Other views distinguished between the EIA as a process and the EIS as the resulting report. Both EIA and EIS include the assessment of impacts, as well as measures to mitigate the impacts.

It was observed that guidelines should not be over-prescriptive. There should be guidelines, but it should be made clear that these were a minimum expectation of content and quality. The guidelines do, however, need to be somewhat distinct between habitat/substrate types. And, importantly, they can help ensure some minimum level of comparability among assessments. It was noted that a number of documents were available, both for general EIAs, and DSM in particular, that could inform the development of new guidelines. Specific mention was made of US-EPA guidelines, and work done by the Pacific Community (SPC) and the NIWA on EIS template guidelines and best-practice scientific research methods.

Recommended Actions

Recommendations for Urgent Action (by mid-2017)

General
- A Zero draft of the Strategic Environmental Regulations (SERs) must be drafted as a matter of urgency. If necessary, the commissioning of a consultant for this purpose should be pursued. The SERs should be considered by the LTC and circulated to stakeholders for comment prior to the 2017 Annual Session. Those comments should then inform the draft that is presented to Council for consideration at the annual session in 2017. It was suggested to take advantage of the Berlin Workshop in January 2017.
- The Environmental Assessment & Management provisions of the SERs should be further developed by the LTC and circulated to stakeholders for comment prior to the annual session in 2017. Those comments should then inform the draft that is presented to Council for consideration at the annual session in 2017.
- It was stressed that both the assessment of application for contracts for exploitation and associated EIAs, as well as the development and review of any SEAs, SEMPs and REMPs will involve a substantial increase in the workload of the LTC. It is crucial that adequate funding and personnel be available to cope with this. Once exploitation begins the ISA will need to change, fundamentally, the way it does business to reflect its role as a major day-to-day mining regulator of mineral resources of the Area. This is considered in the context of the Article 154 Review process.

WG1: Definitions
- Definitions will need special attention in the early stages of crafting the regulations but will also need to evolve throughout the process. See **Annex I** for a platform for moving definitions forward.

WG2-1: Best available scientific evidence
- The ISA should review its capacity to evaluate the status of BAS in contractor reports. Criteria for meeting international standards (in terms of best agreed scientific practices) should be addressed. Peer review is commonly used, but is not always necessarily adequate; therefore, independent and external review should be part of the process (1 year, ongoing).
- The LTC should review how it views modelling results as these can be based on variable data. It was agreed that models should not be discounted but assessed for adequacy (for example data input adequacy, validation methods, ground-truth surveys, model type). Criteria should be established for the acceptability of modelling in EIAs (1 year).
- The LTC produces scientific guidelines every five years. However, there is a recent SPC-NIWA report (the Regional Scientific Research Guidelines which incorporates many ISA guidelines) that prescribes best practices for carrying out scientific research as part of prospecting and exploration and baseline/monitoring studies. The LTC should review this report and consider using it to update the ISA Recommendations for the Guidance of Contractors on baseline studies (1 year).
- The ISA should consider being more transparent in its decisions and make work plans available to the public (for example for environmental sampling). This would ensure appropriate feedback on whether BAS is being used (ongoing).

WG2-2: Precautionary Approach

- There is a need to scale up marine scientific research to address regional scale environmental issues.
- There is a need to create conditions/requirements for contractors to cooperate in sharing environmental data.
- The ISA must ensure that measures for the protection of vulnerable marine ecosystems are adopted before exploration and exploitation work, which may harm them, is authorized. Criteria may be needed and it could be based on modifying the FAO deep-sea guidelines, as well as establishing appropriate national definitions, as a starting point.
- Transparency must be established by publishing environmental baseline and monitoring data, EIA and SEA reports, meeting reports and/or minutes.
- There is a need to specify which scientific, technical, and value considerations as well as uncertainties inform any particular decision.
- There is a need to establish criteria to evaluate whether an application for an exploration or exploitation contract provides for the 'effective protection and preservation of the marine environment including, but not restricted to, the impact on biodiversity'. This should reflect both best scientific advice and public opinion. This requires a multi-stakeholder workshop which will need funding.
- There is a need to establish requirements for the transparent and independent review of EIAs.
- There is a need to provide clear contractual terms that establish clear thresholds and triggers for monitoring, compliance and verification; including steps to be taken if monitoring shows that harm above the specified threshold will be exceeded.

WG2-3: Transparency, access to information, and public participation

- The ISA needs to build capacity now to share information already available from exploration. This will require consideration of:
  - a clear plan (time-bound and implementable)
  - housing of data: what is the role for ISA? Could the non-confidential exploration / exploitation data be housed cooperatively with another international body? A "clearing house mechanism" sensu CBD or the UN PrepCom? Should we use existing structures like OBIS, etc., or is it justifiable to create a new [ISA] data management structure?
- Recognizing the draft ISA communications strategy currently under discussion, there is still an urgent need for an ISA strategy on multi-stakeholder and wider public engagement / participation. The 2015 Assembly's request was broader than just communications.

WG2-4: Ecosystem-based approach

- When the review of the CCZ management plan is being prepared, adding a 10th APEI to the east should be considered.
- Review management of existing information/data, with specific emphasis on information sharing (transparency) and ensuring the different data sets held by the ISA can be integrated to inform the ISA's understanding of regional-scale environments and ecosystems.

WG3: Strategic Environment Assessment and Strategic Environment Plans

- The ISA needs to develop an overall strategic environmental plan for the CCZ and therefore authorize a RfP process this July 2016. The aim is to deliver the SEAP in 2018. An SEA is necessary for the contractors to start on their EIA.

WG4: Regional Environmental Assessment and Regional Environmental Management Plan

- The ISA should support a global fund for ocean science at the UN in August 2016.
- The ISA needs to establish, with urgency, a regional environmental assessment process and REMPs with input from contractors, the scientific community and other stakeholders. Contractors, scientists and regional organizations are likely to provide important data on other users and potential conflicts between users in the area. (Note: REMPs need to be reviewed periodically with a similar set of inputs).
- The ISA needs to develop regional REAs and REMPs in respect of the three types of mineral resources.

WG5: Risk Assessment

- In order to do ERA at the regional/resource level, it was suggested that a consultant be contracted through request for proposal rather than the staging of workshops. The industry has limited capacity for workshops.
- Guidance from ISA required for: data sharing to inform an ERA; providing more detail on the requirements for an ERA (when and how it should be done); and guidance for exploitation regulations to improve consistency of ERA approach (1-2 years).
- ISA to provide support for projects to target identified gaps in information required for successful ERA (1-2 years).

WG6: Serious Harm to the Marine Environment

- There is an urgent need to carry out a:
  - Consultant study regarding definition of 'serious harm' (and related concepts);
  - Consultant study regarding definition and thresholds for 'substantial evidence'; and
  - Prepare a Technical Expert Working Paper regarding guidelines for provision of information relating to irreversible damage.

WG7: EIA Process

- Scoping and EIA content must be in place as soon as possible to provide contractors with a reasonable level of certainty. The processing of scoping documents and EIAs must be timely.

WG8: Adaptive Management

- To assist the LTC to determine whether AM is appropriate for deep seabed mining and to be incorporated into the Regulations, the Group suggested that preparation of a working definition of AM and AM guidelines would facilitate this decision.

WG9: EIA decision-making process

- Capacity and functioning of the ISA should be considered. The substance should drive the form: once the decision-making process steps are set, the capacity and functioning can be adapted to it (cf. meeting cycles), not the other way around. This is to be considered urgently.

WG10: EIS Template
- ISA needs to clarify geographical and jurisdictional extent of the required EIA/EIS, and whether it includes national jurisdiction(s).

WG11: EIS Guidelines
- The ISA could consider the NIWA EIA template guidelines as a starting point in evaluating the type of document to be developed to complement the EIS template.

Recommendations for short-term action (2-3 years)

WG2-1: Best Available Scientific Evidence
- There should be a detailed research plan included as part of the work plan submitted by a contractor. This "inception science plan" is to specify the types of studies, and the gear and methods to be used. This would enable the LTC to evaluate the level of BAS that might be achieved, and its review can be reflected in the contractor's five-year plan (to be in place 2-3 years).
- There should be an external review of science programmes.

WG2-2: Precautionary Approach
- Establish criteria to evaluate whether an application for an exploration or exploitation contract provides for 'effective protection and preservation of the marine environment including, but not restricted to, the impact on biodiversity'. This must reflect best scientific advice and public opinion on the values placed on minerals, biodiversity and deep sea ecosystems;
- Establish requirements for the transparent and independent review of EIAs;
- Provide clear contractual terms that establish clear thresholds and triggers for monitoring, compliance and verification; including steps to be taken if monitoring shows that harm above specific threshold will be exceeded;
- Improve public participation, for example, through access to meetings for observers, an Ombudsperson for present and future generations, further stakeholder surveys, and utilizing external surveys that capture public opinion regarding the acceptability of risks and the values placed on minerals, biodiversity, and ecosystem services.

WG2-3: Transparency, access to information, and public participation
- There is a need for (i) guidelines / process to determine confidentiality of data and (ii) guidelines/ process to respect that confidentiality in the context of an EIA process.
    - Technical details are *a priori* confidential, whereas environmental data are *a priori* non-confidential. There will, however, be grey areas relating to how confidentiality is determined. Accepting the position of most contractors that all information submitted to LTC is confidential would result in potential investors not having access to the information they need.
- ISA should develop an in-house process (i.e. not just the Seabed Disputes Chamber of ITLOS) to resolve potential conflicts / disputes concerning confidentiality / access to data.
- EIA rules will need to be developed with regard to access to information, bearing in mind what will allow for "effective" public participation.
    - Access to (most) information used in the EIA is a basic prerequisite for meaningful and effective public participation.

- o Treatment of public participation comments needs to be procedurally clear.
- o All comments should be clearly captured. Not every individual comment needs to be addressed, but comments can be grouped together by themes.
- o If a given input is viewed as irrelevant, this needs to be noted with a rationale.
- o Although public input has been small to date, it could dramatically increase.
- o Two principles: common heritage of mankind (CHM) vs rights of an "affected" public. CHM suggests broad inclusion.
- o Guidelines are required to determine level of access granted to various groups, for example stakeholders / bodies vs the general public.
- Some info in an EIA assessment can be treated as confidential.

WG2-4: Ecosystem-based approach
Recommendations are as follows to:

- Set specific ecosystem protection and preservation objectives/obligations for regions and/or areas including collection of baseline data and ongoing monitoring;
- Develop ecosystem management plans for areas/regions (REMPs), initially based on information collected prior to approving exploitation contracts, but also to be reviewed based on information gathered during exploitation;
- Develop guidance for contractors regarding what data are to be collected in accordance with an ecosystem-based approach; and the form in which those data should be provided to the ISA to assist with the integrated management of data;
- Develop guidance for contractors regarding the extent of information/data required, and the form in which those data should be provided, to allow integrated management of different sets of data provided by different contractors to the ISA.

WG3: Strategic Environmental Assessment & Strategic Environmental Management Plan
- A SEA is necessary for the contractors to start on their EIA. Therefore, it is envisaged by the group that the SEA should be ready in two to three years. This would require the ISA to
  - o ask external service providers for a quotation/proposal for the first part of the SEA;
  - o build internal capacity that would eventually become the mining inspectorate (see Article 154 Review).

Both items require the necessary budgets to be allocated as of 2017 onwards.

WG4: Regional Environmental Assessment and Regional Environmental Management Plan
- The ISA Secretariat should produce a document detailing the elements to be included in generic REA and REMP based on the consultation and advice from an expert group.
- Consider designing an overarching Strategic Framework for deep-sea mining as a whole that can be applied globally, including Recommendations on elements to be included in an REA and an REMP. The UK Aggregates REMP criteria will be useful here.
- Develop a method of screening for determining major issues to be included in each REMP.
- Encourage greater efforts in understanding the genetic connection of populations, biological distributions in relation to primary productivity, including seasonal and inter-annual variability, and habitat prediction modeling using proxies.

- Clarify the process to be observed in addressing potential conflicts or interference between the conduct of marine scientific research in contractors' areas.
- Clarify the legal status of EMPs in the mining code.
- Create a protocol for accessing data from other organizations for the REA, including issues of different access rights.
- Look at how water column and benthic environments can be integrated and considered in REAs and REMPs.
- Recognize that comprehensive REAs will require assessment of impacts from uses other than mining and that the effectiveness of REMPs may be influenced by these other users, how will the continued coordination with other users be integrated into REA/REMP preparation and implementation? For example, does the ISA need to complete signing MoUs with regional seas organizations?
- Look at whether the REA should regulate cumulative impacts by several contractors working in the same general area and whether this is needed taking into account the size of the license areas and protected areas.

WG7: EIA Process
- Capacity and structural changes must be in place within three to four years and new budgetary obligations to undertake the recommended actions be developed by the Finance Committee.

WG10: EIS Template
- ISA should develop a repository of relevant EIA legislation (both international and of member states) and provide to contractors.
- ISA should advise contractors on how to identify appropriate stakeholders for consultation purposes (develop contact list).
- ISA should clarify the language(s) in which an EIS report is to be submitted and the responsibility for providing translations. ISA should produce a template in the six official languages of the ISA.
- There should be linkages between EIS and an SEA/REMP.

Recommendations for medium-term action (5 years)

WG2-1: Best Available Scientific Evidence
- The science basis for evaluating whether restoration/rehabilitation of marine habitats as a feasible or realistic management objective is poorly developed. This issue should be discussed more widely across mineral resources and deep sea environments (A workshop should be conducted within 5 years).

WG3: Strategic Environmental Assessment and Strategic Environmental Management Plan
- Capacity-building for monitoring/compliance is important for the ISA.

WG4: Regional Environmental Assessment and Regional Environmental Management Plan
- The ISA needs to develop REAs and REMPs for international waters in: (1) the Mid-Atlantic Ridge in the South and North Atlantic; (2) the Indian Ocean ridges; (3) the Indian Ocean polymetallic nodule zone and (4) the seamount clusters for cobalt crust mining in the Western Pacific and Southwest Atlantic.

Annex I: Working Group 1 - Definitions

Guidance by the Working Group on Definitions to assist the LTC in developing the draft regulatory framework in regard to the topic of the working session

- It was agreed that there should be some working definitions of terms listed in the agenda. Some of the terms below were addressed specifically in working groups and are treated in the body of this Report.
- Timing: definitions should be agreed sooner rather than later but certain concepts, in particular, the principles, may lend themselves more to considering the operationalization of those concepts rather than definitions,
- Any definitions should be allowed to evolve over the process of developing the Exploitation Regulations. It was important not to spend too much on definitions in the beginning, as discussions on content would inform the definitions.

A) What is the distinction between EIA / Environmental and social impact assessment?

- There was an agreement that both social and environmental impacts should be considered but it should be clearly specified if the term EIA is to include social considerations. The term could also be ESIA although that would have to be revisited.
- For the purposes of this workshop, the terms EIA and EIs were used with an understanding that social impacts were included. When looking at the EIS template, it should be checked to make sure it also looks at social impacts.

B) Environmental Impact Assessment (EIA)

- MIDAS definition of EIA: 'The technique used to identify and assess the potential impacts of a proposed activity on the environment. For deep sea mining an individual EIA might focus on a specific zone to be mined within a wider contract area as opposed to attempting to assess the effects of mining the whole contract over decadal time scales.'
- There was agreement that a general definition of EIA should take into account the first sentence of the MIDAS definition but also consider generally accepted definitions of EIAs from other regimes. (ISA may wish to look at other regimes to achieve consistent definitions of terms across regimes, where appropriate).
- It was felt that the second part of the MIDAS definition of EIA was more suited to amplification in the EIA process, rather than be included in the definition as this could constrain the process of designing the EIA system.
- The term "environment" could be defined to include social and cultural aspects[2] but t it should be contextualized for the specific purpose of EIAs, bearing in mind that the term "marine environment" was broadly used in the LOS Convention.

---

[2] Indigenous peoples have cultural associations with the sea and its life forms as well as social in the sense of passage, discovery, settlement. They have notions that land water and sea are not inanimate but have familial associations as in Earth Mother, sky father.

C) Environmental Impact Statement (EIS)

- There was some confusion as to whether the EIS is the outcome document of the environmental impact assessment (a process) i.e. the EIA report, or a separate document altogether.
- There was some agreement that an EIS should not only describe the potential impacts but also contain options for mitigation to provide information additional to the EIA. There was a suggestion that the element of evaluation should be included in the definition in addition to the description element.

D) Strategic environmental assessment (SEA)/strategic environmental management plan / regional environmental assessment/regional environmental management plan (REMP)

- There was confusion as to the meaning of these terms.
- The following issues were discussed without arriving at a conclusion:
  - o What do we mean by 'region' in the context of the Area?
  - o There was a question as to whether SEAs addressed policies, plans or measures; and REMPs addressed the variety of activities in a region? There was no agreement.

E) Impact Reference Zones/ Preservation Reference Zones

- MIDAS definitions for PRZ/IRZ do not follow the definitions in the Mining Code. It was agreed to use the definitions in the Mining Code for this workshop.

F) Impact

- The term 'impact' is used in different contexts (impact reference zone; impact zone). Any definition of 'impact' will need to be checked to ensure that it fits these contexts.
- Impact may refer to environmental, social, cultural, and economic impacts. However, there was some disagreement regarding the inclusion of economic impacts.
- The Recommendations for the Guidance of Contractors for assessment of possible environmental impacts define an "impact zone" as a "Zone where impacts (direct, indirect, cumulative and/or interactive result from the activity."
- In addition to the existing definition, one suggestion was made for defining environmental impact which was not discussed in detail: "Environmental impact" means any effect from exploitation activities on the marine environment, including social considerations and human health, being positive, negative, direct, indirect, temporary or permanent, or cumulative arising over time or in combination with other effects.'
- Attention was also drawn to the definition in the Espoo Convention: "'Impact" means any effect caused by a proposed activity on the environment including human health and safety, flora, fauna, soil, air, water, climate, landscape and historical monuments or other physical structures or the interaction among these factors; it also includes effects on cultural heritage or socio-economic conditions resulting from alterations to those factors.'

G) Environmental Impact Zone / Far field impact zone

- There was a lot of discussion on how to define an impact area.
- It is important to distinguish between IRZ and impact area. IRZ is a predefined term of an area that should be representative of the ecological characteristics of the mine zone. The impact zone is scientifically defined based on the evidence that is collected, i.e. the zone in which the impacts occur. Both zones exist in parallel.
- For the impact zone, there is no need to define the zone precisely. We can simply say that the size of the impact zone is determined by the area in which impacts occur. This might include zones outside a contractor's area. The contractor, while bearing in mind the issue of potentially entering another contractor's area, must monitor the entire impact zone.

H) Best environmental practices (BEP)

- There was some discussion as to what BEP includes:
    o BEP may include other principles, such as applying a precautionary approach.
    o BEP are not static and must be flexible to incorporate new standards.
    o A concern is that operators may not be able to change practices at short intervals as their operations need to be economically viable.

I) Intergenerational equity

- No tangible outcome and direction emerged from discussion.

J) Precautionary approach

- There was some agreement that we should not define approaches, such as precaution, but rather focus on how to operationalize them.

K) Transparency / Public Participation

- It was noted that this was missing from the list of principles, although it was included in the working group on sharing of information.

Actions Suggested by the Working Group of Definitions

- Definitions would need special attention in the early stages of crafting the regulations but would also need to evolve throughout the process.
- Definitions should strive to reflect the particular situation of exploitation as well as be consistent, to the extent possible, with existing definitions.

Annex II: Environmental Assessment Flowcharts and Process Options

1.   Flowchart of the EIA decision-making process

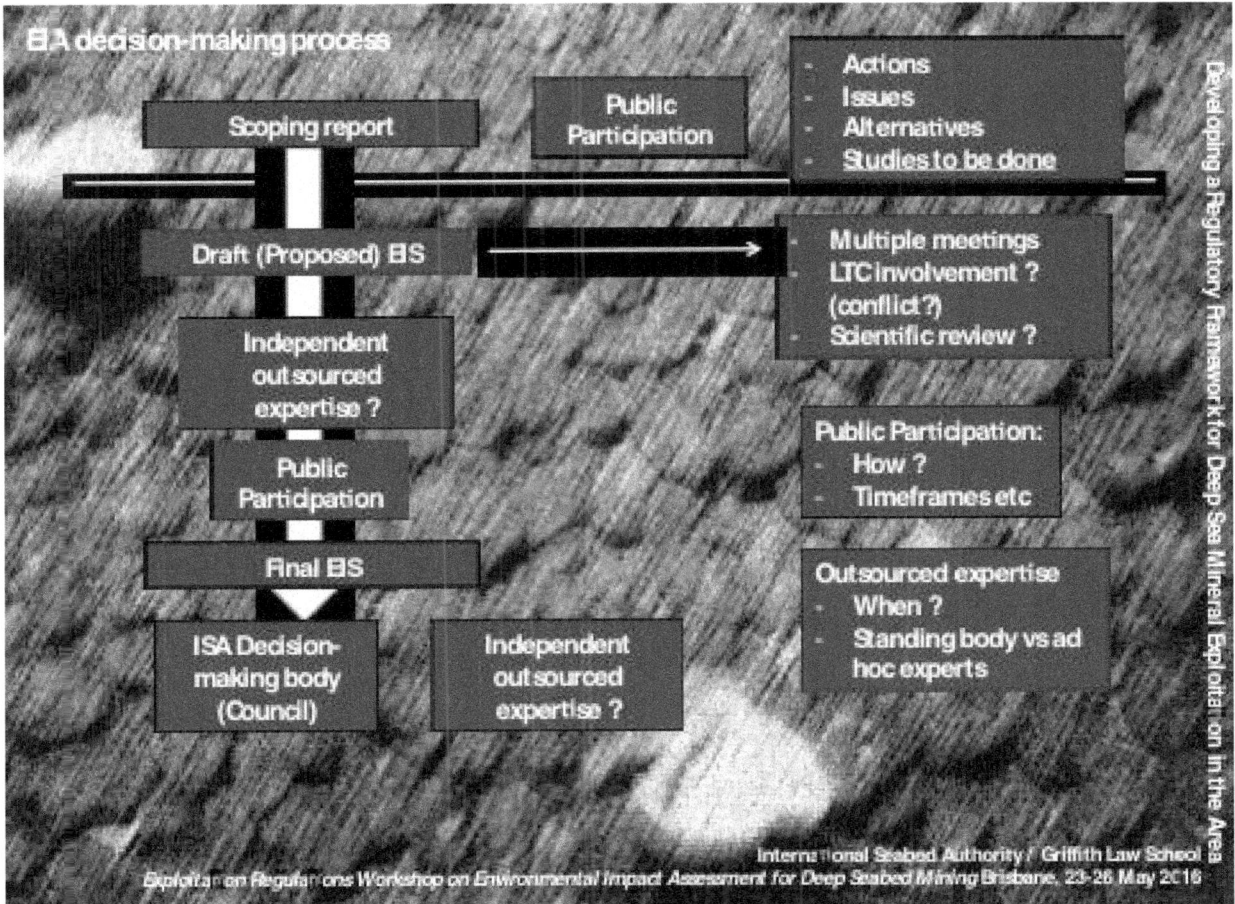

2. *Environmental Assessment Process Options (Flowchart Examples)*

Convention on Biological Diversity / Ramsar Convention
(from UNEP/CBD/SBSTTA/7/13 and Ramsar Wise Use Handbook 11)

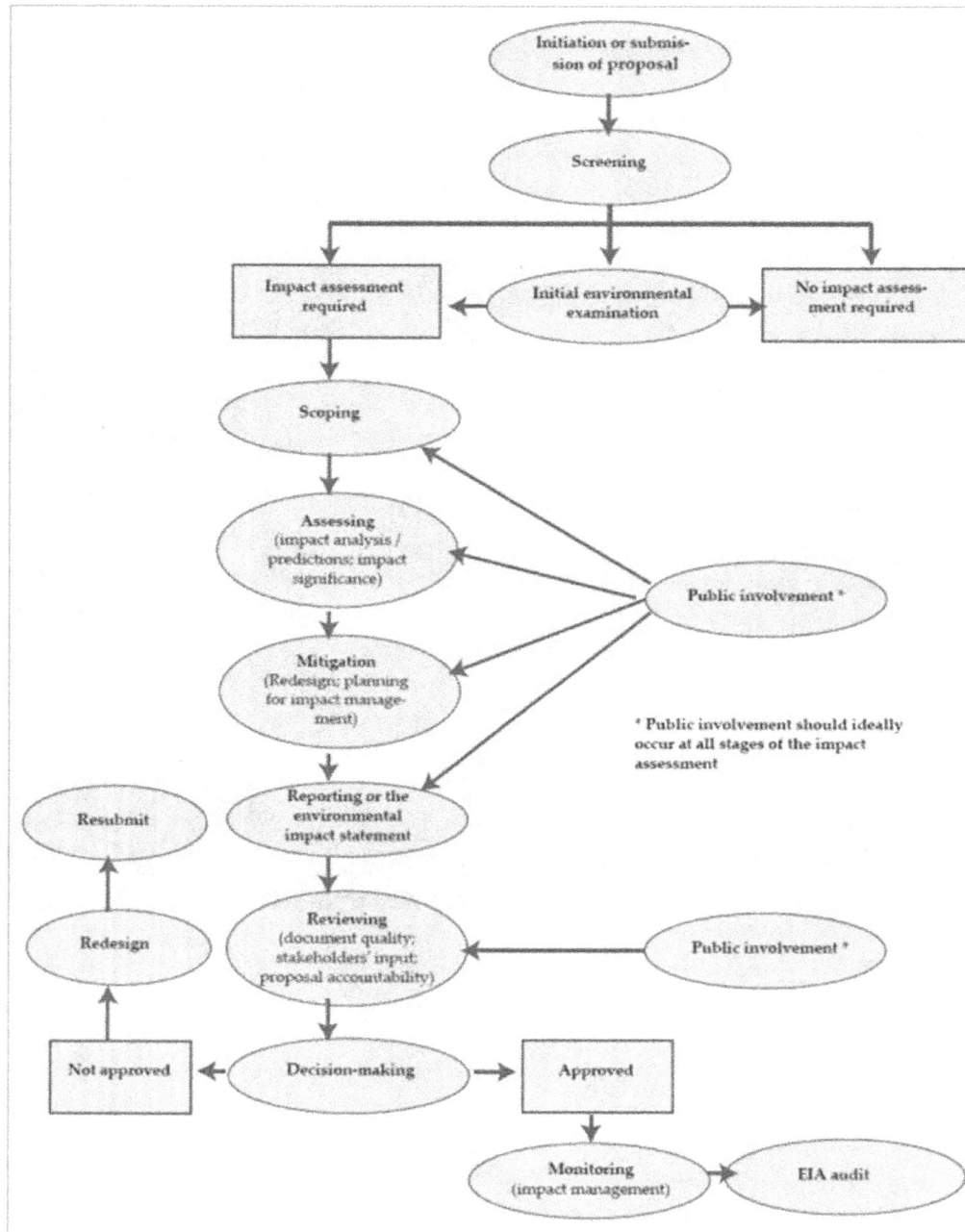

Generalised EIA
Process Flowchart

```
                          ┌──────────────────┐
                          │    Proposal      │
                          │  Identification  │
                          └──────────────────┘
                                   │
                            ┌────────────┐
                            │ Screening  │
                            └────────────┘
                                   │
        ┌──────────────────────────┼──────────────────────────┐
        │                          │                          │
┌──────────────┐         ┌──────────────────┐         ┌──────────────┐
│ EIA Required │◄────────│     Initial      │────────►│   No EIA     │
└──────────────┘         │  environmental   │         └──────────────┘
        │                │   examination    │
┌──────────────┐         └──────────────────┘         ┌──────────────────┐
│   Scoping    │◄──────────────────────────────────── │ *Public involvement │
└──────────────┘                                       └──────────────────┘
        │
┌──────────────────┐
│ Impact analysis  │
└──────────────────┘
        │
┌──────────────────┐
│   Mitigation     │
│   and impact     │
│   management     │
└──────────────────┘
        │
┌──────────────┐
│  EIA Report  │
└──────────────┘
        │
┌──────────────┐                                       ┌──────────────────┐
│   Review     │◄──────────────────────────────────── │ *Public involvement │
└──────────────┘                                       └──────────────────┘
```

*Public involvement typically occurs at these points. It may also occur at any other stage of the EIA Process.

```
┌──────────────┐
│  Resubmit    │
└──────────────┘
┌──────────────┐      ┌──────────────────┐
│  Redesign    │      │ Decision-making  │
└──────────────┘      └──────────────────┘
        │              │               │
┌──────────────┐   ┌──────────────┐
│ Not approved │   │  Approved    │
└──────────────┘   └──────────────┘
                        │
             ┌──────────────────────┐
             │ Implementation and   │
             │     follow up        │
             └──────────────────────┘
```

Information from this process contributes to effective future EIA

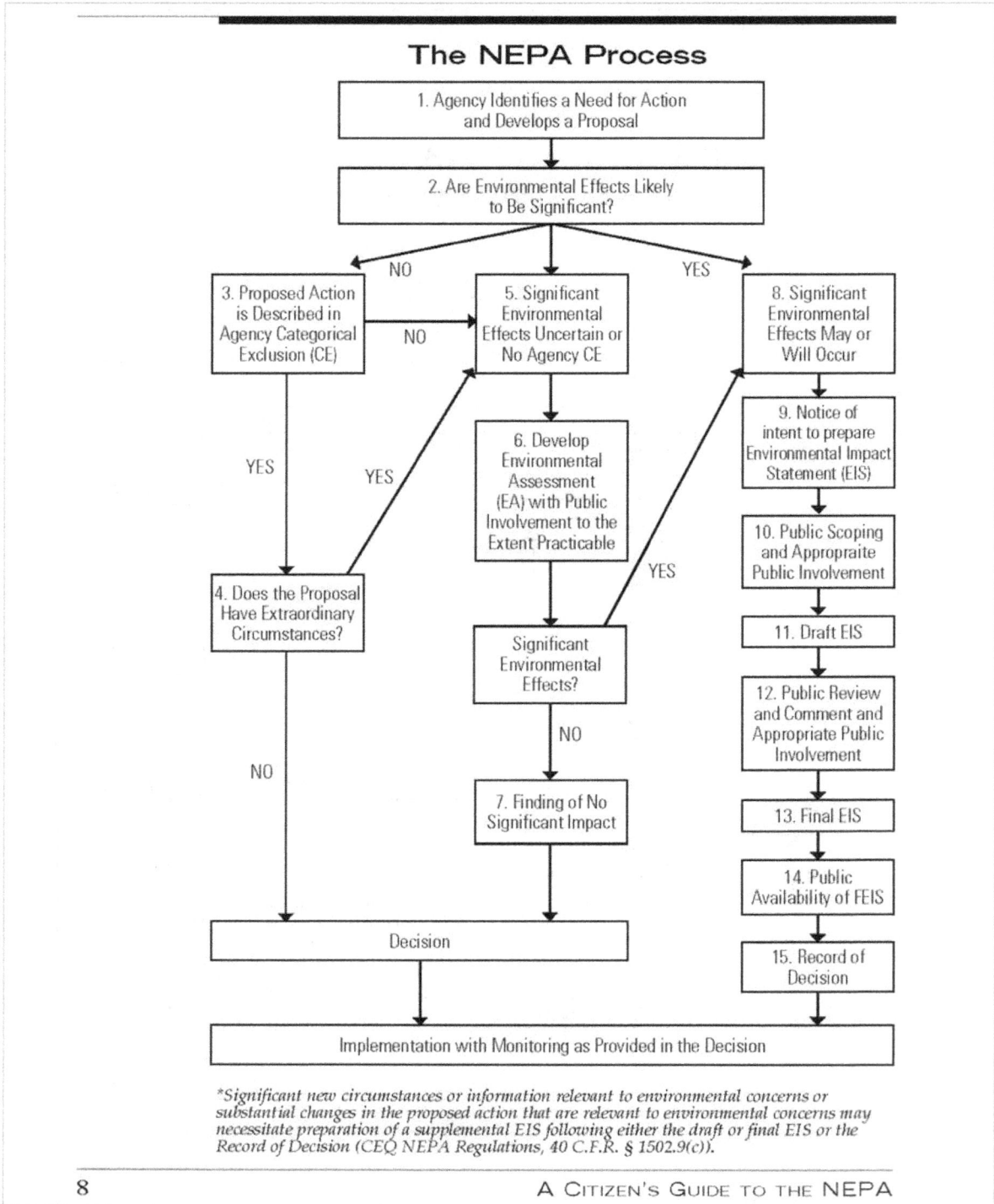

U.S. National Environmental Policy Act, 1969

The NEPA Process

1. Agency Identifies a Need for Action and Develops a Proposal

2. Are Environmental Effects Likely to Be Significant?

— NO —   — YES —

3. Proposed Action is Described in Agency Categorical Exclusion (CE)

NO →

5. Significant Environmental Effects Uncertain or No Agency CE

8. Significant Environmental Effects May or Will Occur

YES

YES

6. Develop Environmental Assessment (EA) with Public Involvement to the Extent Practicable

9. Notice of intent to prepare Environmental Impact Statement (EIS)

10. Public Scoping and Appropraite Public Involvement

4. Does the Proposal Have Extraordinary Circumstances?

YES

Significant Environmental Effects?

11. Draft EIS

12. Public Review and Comment and Appropriate Public Involvement

NO

NO

7. Finding of No Significant Impact

13. Final EIS

14. Public Availability of FEIS

Decision

15. Record of Decision

Implementation with Monitoring as Provided in the Decision

Significant new circumstances or information relevant to environmental concerns or substantial changes in the proposed action that are relevant to environmental concerns may necessitate preparation of a supplemental EIS following either the draft or final EIS or the Record of Decision (CEQ NEPA Regulations, 40 C.F.R. § 1502.9(c)).

8

A CITIZEN'S GUIDE TO THE NEPA

Western Australia EIA Administrative Procedures Act, 2010

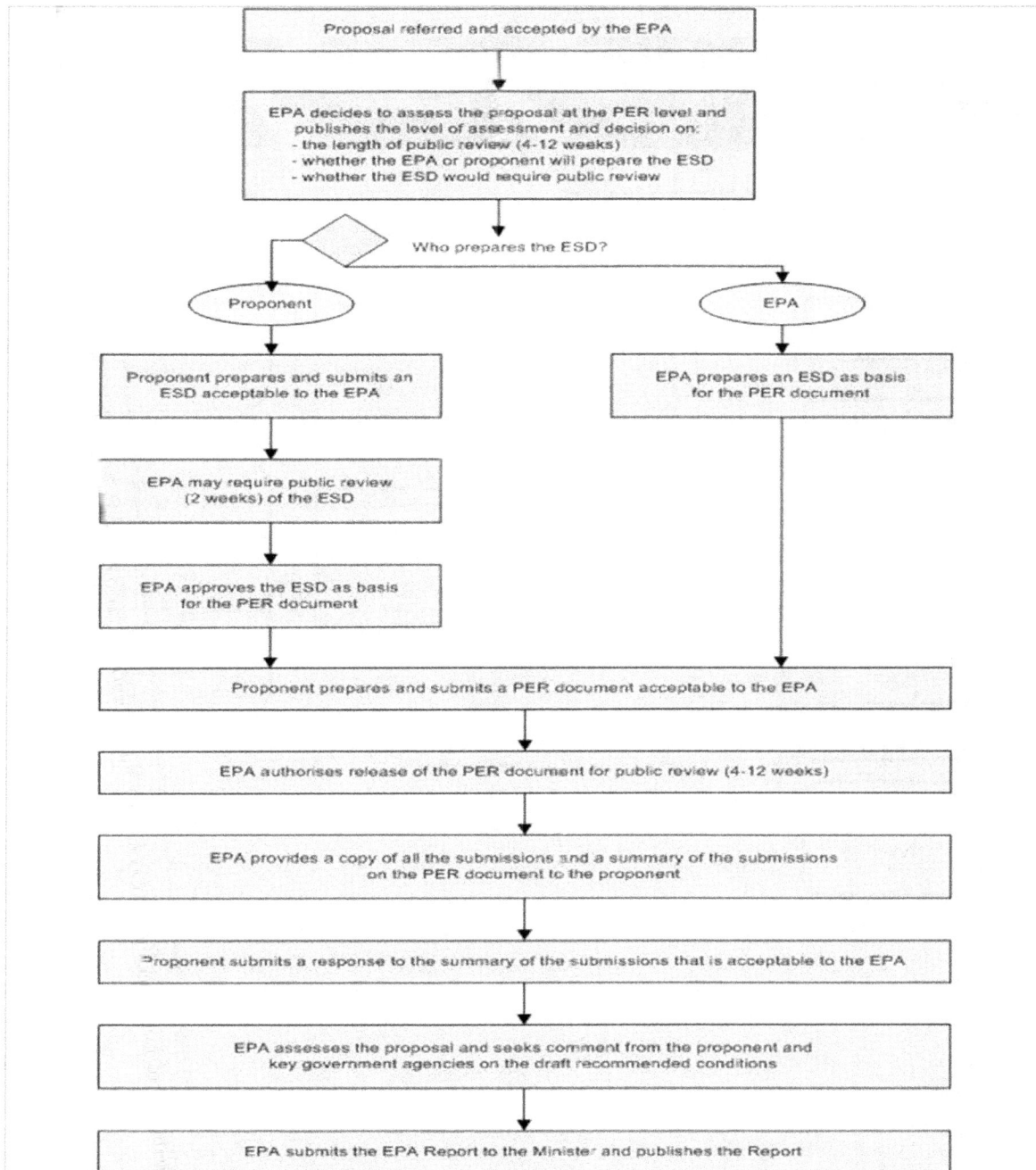

45 | P a g e</>

Canadian Environmental Assessment Act, 2012 (particularly steps 2-4)

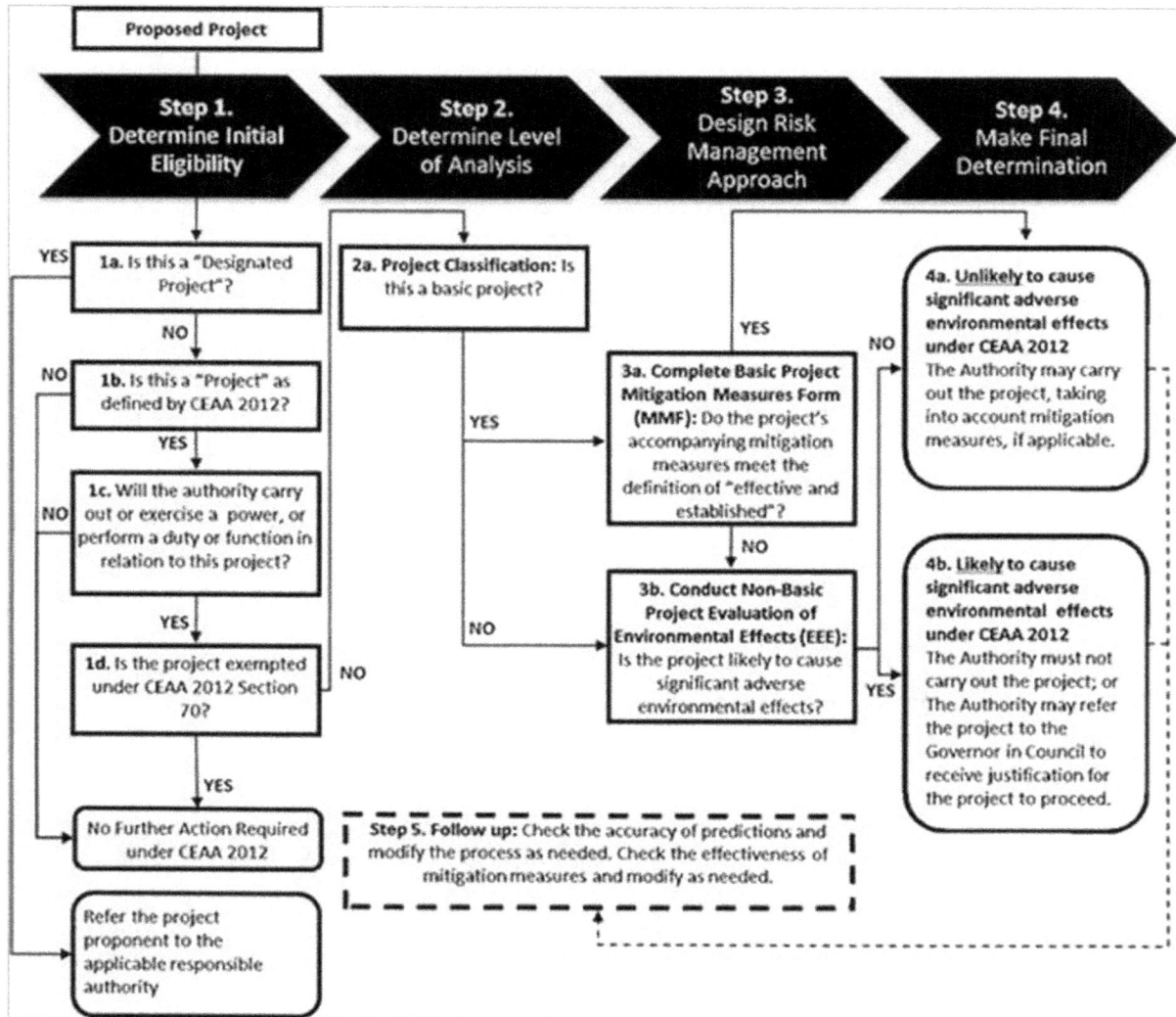

Flowchart:

Proposed Project →

Step 1. Determine Initial Eligibility | **Step 2. Determine Level of Analysis** | **Step 3. Design Risk Management Approach** | **Step 4. Make Final Determination**

Step 1:
- **1a.** Is this a "Designated Project"? — YES (branch); NO ↓
- **1b.** Is this a "Project" as defined by CEAA 2012? — NO (branch); YES ↓
- **1c.** Will the authority carry out or exercise a power, or perform a duty or function in relation to this project? — NO (branch); YES ↓
- **1d.** Is the project exempted under CEAA 2012 Section 70? — NO (branch); YES ↓
- No Further Action Required under CEAA 2012
- Refer the project proponent to the applicable responsible authority

Step 2:
- **2a. Project Classification:** Is this a basic project? — YES → 3a; NO → 3b

Step 3:
- **3a. Complete Basic Project Mitigation Measures Form (MMF):** Do the project's accompanying mitigation measures meet the definition of "effective and established"? — YES → 4a; NO ↓
- **3b. Conduct Non-Basic Project Evaluation of Environmental Effects (EEE):** Is the project likely to cause significant adverse environmental effects? — NO → 4a; YES → 4b

Step 4:
- **4a. Unlikely** to cause significant adverse environmental effects under CEAA 2012
  The Authority may carry out the project, taking into account mitigation measures, if applicable.
- **4b. Likely** to cause significant adverse environmental effects under CEAA 2012
  The Authority must not carry out the project; or The Authority may refer the project to the Governor in Council to receive justification for the project to proceed.

Step 5. Follow up: Check the accuracy of predictions and modify the process as needed. Check the effectiveness of mitigation measures and modify as needed.

Annex III: Environmental Impact Statement Template [Work In Progress]

Draft ISA Environmental Impact Statement template

1. **Table of Contents**
2. **Glossary and abbreviations**

3. **Executive Summary**
 	
One of the main objectives of this section is to provide an explanation of the project for non-technical readers. Information provided in the executive summary should briefly describe:
 	
    3.1. **The proposed development activity and its objectives**
 	
    3.2. **Anticipated bio-physical and socio-economic impacts (direct/indirect, reversible/irreversible) of the activity**
 	
    3.3. **Details of remedial actions that are proposed**
 	
    3.4. **The benefits to be derived from the project**
 	
    3.5. **Details of the consultation programme undertaken by the applicant, including degree of public interest**
 	
    3.6. **End-use plans for the development activity – decommissioning etc.**
 	
The summary should not be more than 15 pages in length, in the six official languages of the United Nations.

4. **Study team**
 	
This section should outline all people involved in carrying out the Environmental Impact Assessment (EIA) studies and writing the EIA report.
 	
    4.1. **Proponent**
 	
    4.2. **Lead environmental consultant(s)**
 	
    4.3. **EIS specialist sub-consultants**
 	
Copies of CVs and qualifications should be included as an annex.

5. Introduction

5.1. Background

This section should briefly summarize the project being proposed. Including all activities and locations.

5.2. Project purpose and need

The purpose of this section is to ensure that only development activities that are in line with the country's goals and objectives are considered for approval. This section should provide information on the viability of the proposed development. Include economic context, why the project is needed, benefits to sponsoring state (in line with common heritage of mankind).

5.3. Project history

This section should briefly summarize the work undertaken up to the date the EIA Report was finalized and ready to be submitted. This should include a brief description of the deposit discovery, the exploration and test mining activities conducted to date.

5.3.1 Technical
5.3.2 Environmental
5.3.3 Social

This should include a general description of stakeholder consultation

5.4. Project proponent

This section should summarize the credentials of the mining company proposing the development including major shareholders, other tenements owned, and their jurisdictions, etc. The proponent's technological and environmental expertise, capacity and resources should be outlined.

5.5. This report

5.5.1. Scope

Based on earlier assessment or work, detail what is and what is not included based on earlier assessments or work. Link to other supporting information.

5.5.2. Report structure

This section is required if the EIA Report spans multiple volumes (documents) and can provide additional details not listed in the main report's table of contents.

6. Policy, legal and administrative framework

This section should provide information on relevant legislation, agreements or policies that are applicable to the proposed mining operation.

6.1. Applicable mining and environmental legislation, policy and agreements

The applicant should note any national legislation, regulation or guidelines that apply to the management or regulation of seabed mining. This should include a note on how the proposed operation will comply with these requirements.

6.2. Other applicable legislation, policy and regulations

Description of any other legislation, policy or regulations that do not apply specifically to seabed mining or environment, but may be relevant to the proposal (e.g. shipping regulations, offshore mining certificates, Maritime declaration, foreign investment, marine scientific research, occupational health and safety, climate change etc.).

6.3. Relevant international and regional agreements

This subsection should list all international agreements applicable to the operation, such as UNCLOS,[3] CBD,[4] the IMO suite of environmental and safety conventions, SOLAS, MARPOL, the London Convention and Protocol, Noumea Convention,[5] Apia Convention,[6] etc. that the State is party to.

6.4. International and regional standards, principles and guidelines

Any other non-legally-binding standards or guidelines that may apply to best practice in the operation, e.g. Equator Principles,[7] Madang Guidelines,[8] IMMS Code,[9] ISA guidelines,[10] IFC Performance Standards,[11] etc.

7. Stakeholder consultation and disclosure

This section describes all consultation(s) that have taken place with interested parties and stakeholders whom have an interest in the proposed DSM activity in the period leading up to the application.

7.1. Consultation requirements

This outlines any international consultation obligations.

7.2. Stakeholders

List any relevant stakeholders or other interested parties that have been consulted and explain how stakeholders were identified.

---

[3] http://www.un.org/depts/los/convention_agreements/texts/unclos/closindx.htm
[4] http://www.cbd.int/convention/text/
[5] http://www.sprep.org/legal/the-convention
[6] http://www.sprep.org/legal/meetings-apia-convention
[7] http://www.equator-principles.com/resources/equator_principles_III.pdf
[8] http://ict.sopac.org/VirLib/MR0362.pdf
[9] http://www.immsoc.org/IMMS_downloads/2011_SEPT_15_IMMS_Code.pdf
[10] http://www.isa.org.jm/documents-resources/publications

7.3 Public consultation and disclosure programme

Description of the consultation workshops/meetings that occurred prior to the preparation of the report.

7.3.1. Goals

7.3.2. Methods

7.3.3. Programme/schedule

7.3.4. Scientific workshops and other procedures for independent expert peer review of studies

7.3.5. Cultural heritage

7.3.6. Outcomes

Include a description of key concerns and comments identified by stakeholders and how the proponent intends to address these concerns, or why not.

7.4 Continuing consultation and disclosure

What further consultation with stakeholders is needed and planned?

8. Description of the proposed development

This section should provide all relevant details of the proposed development activity including relevant diagrams and drawings. Details to be provided under this section may include the headings listed below.

8.1. Project area definition

8.1.1. Location

This section should include coordinates of project area, detailed location maps (drawn to scale and how boundaries are expected to change with time), site layout, any closed/ exclusion areas.

8.1.2. Associated activities

This section should include a description of any supporting activities and infrastructure required (e.g. ports, barges, transportation corridors, crew transfers etc.) that are outside the direct mining site.

8.2. Mineral resource

This section should detail the type of resource proposed for extraction (e.g. SMS, MN, CRC etc.), the type of commodity, the grade and volume. Estimates of inferred and indicated resource should be provided. Visual models of the resource should be provided.

8.3. Project Components

This section should provide background information to the proposal.

8.3.1. Mining

This section should include technologies to be employed with relevant diagrams and drawings, and should cover: mine plan, general mining sequence, technologies to be employed to separate the resource from the seabed, depth of penetration into the seabed etc.

8.3.2. Transport/materials handling

Description of all methods from transporting the resource to the surface, and then to the shipment of the resource overseas.

8.3.3. On-site processing

Description of any processing on the seafloor and at the surface including methods to separate the resource from the seawater/fines and the disposal of seawater/fines etc.

8.3.4. Project Scale

Overview of the spatial and temporal scales of the operation including volumes of material to be extracted, processed, and deposited over how extensive of an area.

8.3.5. Support equipment

Describes any equipment expected to be needed for mining and support operations (e.g., mining vessels/platforms, supply vessels, barges). Describe anticipated frequency of vessel movements for support, supply, barge removal etc.

8.4. Hazardous materials management

8.4.1. Description of hazardous materials

8.4.2. Transportation

8.4.3. Storage, handling and disposal

8.5. Commissioning

8.6. Decommissioning

Including offshore infrastructures and onshore facilities.

8.7. Construction and operating standards

This section should outline the design codes to which the equipment will be/is built, as well as the health and safety standards that will be applied.

8.7.1. Design codes

8.7.2. Health and safety

8.8. Workforce

8.8.1. Workforce description

8.8.2. Employment policy

8.8.3. Capacity-building objectives and commitments

8.9. Alternatives considered and rejected from analysis

8.9.1. Site selection process

Information on methods of site selection including alternatives investigated.

8.9.2. Mining production scenarios

      8.9.3.   **Transport/materials handling**

      8.9.4.   **On-site processing**

      8.9.5.   **No-mining alternative**

8.10. Other studies

This includes any other relevant technical studies that have been carried out.

9. Development timetable (Detailed schedule)

Description of the overall timetable, from construction through to decommissioning and closure of operations. This should include the major phases of the operation, as well as the milestone dates on which relevant tasks are expected to be completed. Information on the development timetable provided under this section should clearly communicate the different phases in the development proposal.

For reasons of clarity, a Flow chart / Gantt chart should be used where appropriate.
Information provided should include, but not be limited to, the following:

- The funding arrangement for proposed activity including any conditions or approvals required;
- Pre-construction activities;
- Construction schedule, staging, etc.;
- Commissioning and operational schedules;
- Infrastructure development schedule;
- Rehabilitation;
- Monitoring during operations;
- Closure schedule;

Monitoring post-closure.

10. Description of the existing physico-chemical environment

This section should give a detailed account of knowledge of the environmental conditions at the site. It should include information gleaned from a thorough literature review as well as specially designed on-site studies. It provides the baseline description of the geological and oceanographic conditions.

10.1. Key messages

Overview of key content (can be a box with up to 6 bullet points of the main aspects covered, or the main findings)

10.2. Regional overview

Description of the general environmental conditions of the site, including geological and oceanographic setting within a broader regional context. This is a brief section which should include a map, more detailed site- specific description will be below.

10.3. Studies completed

Description of any prior research/exploration activities that are relevant for this EIA and future activities.

10.4. Special considerations for site

Description of any notable characteristics of the site, such as hydrothermal venting, seamounts, high-surface productivity, eddies etc. Include site specific issues and characteristics, particularly for rare or fragile environments.

10.5. Meteorology and air quality

General overview of climatology, e.g. wind directions and speeds, seasonal patterns. This section may be most relevant to surface operations.

10.6. Geological setting/context

Description of the nature and extent of the mineral deposit and bedrock within its broader geological context. Description of the general geological landscape and topographic features of the site. Maps with high resolution bathymetry.

10.7. Physical oceanographic setting

Description of oceanographic aspects such as currents, sedimentation rates, and waves. Time-series data should be ground-'truthed' to a regional ocean model, and details are required on changes with depth, and between near-field and far-field.

10.8. Water quality

Description of water mass characteristics at the site and at various depths of the water column in particular near the seafloor, including nutrients, particle loads, temperature and dissolved gas profiles, vent fluid characteristics, turbidity and geochemistry etc.

10.9. Seabed Substrate characteristics

Description of substrate composition, including physical and chemical properties (e.g., sediment composition, pore-water profiles, grain size, sediment mechanics).

10.10. Natural Hazards

Description of volcanism, seismic activity, cyclonic trends, tsunamis etc.

10.11. Noise

Description of ambient noise, if any, influence of ongoing exploration and maritime activity.

10.12. Summary of existing physico–chemical environment

Bring together key findings e.g. any sensitive environments or highly valued areas. This will be up to 1 page, and more extensive than the key messages section.

11. Description of existing biological environment

A description of the various biological components and communities that are present in or utilize the water column and seabed in the region of the site. It should include information from a thorough literature review as well as specially designed on-site studies. Include benthic multivariate analysis at appropriate scales with replication, genetic diversity, population structure, megafauna, macrofauna, microfauna, resource-specific fauna, trophic relationships and habitat maps.

11.1. Key messages

Overview of key content (can be a box with up to 6 bullet points of the main aspects covered, or the main findings).

11.2. Regional overview

General regional context. Any previously identified areas meeting the criteria for EBSAS and VMEs. Existing conservation areas, protected species etc. This is a brief section, but provides the broader scale context for the more detailed site-specific description below.

11.3. Studies completed

Description of any prior research/exploration activities that are relevant for this EIA and future activities.

11.4. Biological communities

The format of this section should be structured via depth regime. Diversity, abundance, biomass, connectivity, trophic relationships, resilience, function and temporal variability will need to be addressed. Samples should be from the various habitats, topography, seabed characteristics etc. For SMS, temperature-fauna relationships should also be studied including the 'zone of influence' of the vent system.

11.4.1 Surface

From the surface down to 200 m. This includes plankton (Phytoplankton and zooplankton), surface/near surface fish such as tuna, also seabirds and marine mammals.

11.4.2 Midwater

Open water from a depth of 200m down to 50 m from the seafloor and includes zooplankton, mesopelagic and bathypelagic fishes, deep diving mammals.

11.4.3 Benthic

Invertebrate and fish communities, including infauna and demersal fish up to a height of 50 m above the seafloor

These sections should include sub-sections on:

- **Plankton** (Phytoplankton, zooplankton)
- **Mesopelagic fauna** (fish, squid, macrozooplankton)
- **Fish** (assemblages, pelagic, demersal)
- **Marine mammals** (Cetaceans, pinnipeds)
- **Reptiles** (Turtles)
- **Seabirds**
- **Benthic invertebrates**

The description needs to stress the interactions and linkages between habitats and faunal groups in a 3-D context. This will include description of what depth regimes are relevant, though site specific.

11.5. Summary of existing biological environment

Bring together key findings, e.g. regional distributions, any sensitive environments and fauna or highly valued areas. This will be up to a page, and more extensive than the key messages.

12. Description of existing socio-economic environment[11]

This section should describe the socio-economic significance of the project area.

12.1 Key messages

Overview of key content (can be a box with up to 6 bullet points of the main aspects covered, or the main findings)

12.2 Existing uses

12.1.1. Fisheries

12.1.2. Tourism

This section describes marine cruise liners, game fishing, and other tourism activities

12.1.3. Marine Scientific Research

12.1.4. Marine Protected Areas and Marine Parks

12.1.5. Other

List other uses of the project area that are not related to the above (e.g. telecommunications cables, other mineral exploitation projects, bioprospecting etc.)

12.3 Cultural environment

List places of cultural/historical significance that occur within the zone of influence of the project area (e.g. shipwrecks, traditional fishing grounds, World Heritage Sites etc.)

12.4 Summary of existing socio-cultural environment

Bring together key findings of socio-cultural environment. This will be up to a page, and more extensive than the key messages in the first section.

13. Results of test mining operations (if applicable)

13.1 Description of the test mining activity

Location and scale of operation, non-proprietary description of equipment used and ore recovered.

13.2 Description of impact assessment activities

Sampling equipment, sample types, locations, replication, measurements, monitoring, etc.

13.3 Results of impact assessment activities

Provide overview of results and place full results in an appendix.

---

[11] The revised template further on has some description of EEZ issues that will be removed if necessary. There is a need for a very clear directive from the ISA whether the template/guidelines refer solely to the Area, and not consider interactions with EEZs.

14. Assessment of impacts on physico-chemical environment and proposed mitigation measures

Description and evaluation of potential impacts of the mining operation to the physical environment as previously identified.

14.1 Key messages

14.2 Impact assessment method

Include a description of impact assessment methods e.g., Significance Assessment Method, Risk Assessment Method or Compliance Based Assessment Methods or others (e.g., air quality could be assessed under the compliance method). A conservative approach to impact assessment should be applied.

14.3 Impact categories

This sub-section is an overview and description of general impact categories caused by the mining operation. This is not expected to be detailed, but introduce the major types of effect, such as material removal, creation of sediment plumes, noise, light etc. A description should be included of any lessons learnt from activities during the exploratory phase of the programme (e.g. test mining trials). Include direct, indirect, and cumulative impacts.

14.4 Identification of threats

The format of the subsequent subsections should be consistent between and within sections. Each subsection should include:

    A. The nature and extent of any impact;

    B. Measures that will be taken to avoid, mitigate or minimise such impact; and

    C. What unavoidable impacts will remain (residual impacts).

It is expected that some repetition will occur between sections, notably where an impact of the mining operation will affect several components of the environment at the site.

14.4.1 Meteorology and air quality

Description of potential effect on the air quality from the surface or subsurface operations.

14.4.2 Geological setting

Description of impacts the mining may have on the topography of the site or geological / geophysical composition.

14.4.3 Physical oceanographic setting

Description of effects on current speed/direction, sedimentation rates, etc. Regional oceanographic model will be relevant for this section

14.4.4 Water quality

Description of effects such as sediment plume generation (composition and concentration) and clarity of water, particulate loading, water temperature, dissolved gas and nutrient levels etc., in all levels of the water column.

Regional oceanographic model will be relevant for this section

For SMS, modification of vent fluid discharges should be addressed

14.4.5   Seabed sediment characteristics

For example: changes in the sediment composition, grain size, density, pore water profiles.

14.4.6   Natural hazards

Discussion of any impacts of the operation on natural hazards (any chance of increasing earthquake risk, volcanic activity) and potential impacts of regular natural events on mining operations, and plans for these hazards? e.g. Volcanic eruptions, seismic activity, sea floor instability and tsunami.

14.4.7   Noise

Noise above existing levels

14.4.8   GHGs and climate change

Estimated greenhouse gas emissions released by activities and any activity that may affect water acidity.

14.4.9   Maritime safety and interactions with shipping

Include project safety and interaction with other vessels

14.4.10   Waste management

Vessel waste management, with reference to compliance with relevant conventions, legislation or principles, methods of cleaner production and energy balance.

14.4.11   Cumulative impacts

The nature and extent of any interactions between various impacts, where they may have cumulative effects must be considered. Consideration should be given to cumulative effects of climate change (warming waters, expanding oxygen minimum zones, rising sea levels, increasing acidification etc.) and their potential to interact with and exacerbate DSM impacts.

14.4.11.1   Proposed operations impacts

Cumulative within the scope of the mining proposed herein.

14.4.11.2   Regional operation impacts

Cumulative between activities where known in the region

14.5   Summary of residual effects

15.   Assessment of impacts on biological environment and proposed mitigation measures

This section will focus on aspects of greatest risk to the biological environment.

15.1   Key messages

15.2   Impact assessment method

Include a description of impact assessment methods. i.e. Before EIA is written, an ecological risk assessment (ERA) should be carried out, which will evaluate the likelihood and consequences of the mining operation having an impact on the biological environment. This means the EIA will describe in greater detail the main impacts on the biological environment and less so on elements of minor risks. A conservative approach to impact assessment should be applied.

15.3   Impact categories

This sub-section is an overview and description of general impact categories caused by the mining operation. This is not expected to be detailed, but introduce the major types of effect, such as material removal, creation of sediment plumes, noise, light etc. A description should be included of any lessons learnt from activities during the exploratory phase of the programme (e.g. test mining trials). Include direct, indirect, and cumulative impacts. Include direct, indirect, and cumulative impacts.

15.4 Identification of threats

Using the same structure as Section 11.4, describe the effects on individuals, communities, populations, and meta-populations.

The format of these subsequent subsections should be consistent between and within sections. Each subsection should include:

A.   *The nature and extent of any impact;*

B.   *Measures that will be taken to avoid, mitigate or minimize such impact; and*

C.   *What unavoidable impacts will remain (residual impacts).*

It is expected that some repetition will occur between sections, notably where an impact of the mining operation will affect several components of the environment at the site.

15.4.1   Pelagic

15.4.2   Midwater

15.4.3   Benthic

15.4.4   Biosecurity

Consider need for equipment cleaning between locations. e.g. ballast water issues and ship movement into the area and out for servicing / processing

15.4.5 Cumulative impacts

The nature and extent of any interactions between various impacts, where they may have cumulative effects must be considered.

15.4.5.1 Proposed operations impacts

Cumulative within the scope of the mining proposed herein.

15.4.5.2 Regional operation impacts

Cumulative between activities where known in the region

15.4.6 Other issues

Outline where there are other more general issues, i.e. aspects of existing conservation areas and management plans etc.

15.4.7 Summary of residual effects

16.   Assessment of impacts on the onshore environment and proposed mitigation

16.1   Key messages

16.2 Impact assessment method

16.3 Impact categories

16.4 Identification of threats

For each component identified include:

      A. The nature and extent of any impact;

      B. Measures that will be taken to avoid, mitigate or minimize such impact; and

      C. What unavoidable impacts will remain (residual impacts).

It is expected that some repetition will occur between sections, notably where an impact of the mining operation will affect several components.

16.5 Identification of threats

---

17. Assessment of impacts on socio-economic environment and proposed mitigation

In this section, the applicant is to provide a description and evaluation of potential impacts of the mining operation to previously identified socio-economic components. The format should be consistent between sections.

17.1 Key messages

17.2 Impact assessment method

17.3 Impact categories

17.4 Identification of threats

For each component identified include:

      A. The nature and extent of any impact;

      B. Measures that will be taken to avoid, mitigate or minimize such impact; and

      C. What unavoidable impacts will remain (residual impacts).

It is expected that some repetition will occur between sections, notably where an impact of the mining operation will affect several components.

17.4.1 Existing uses

    17.4.1.1.1 Fisheries

    17.4.1.1.2 Tourism

    17.4.1.1.3 Marine scientific research

    17.4.1.1.4 Marine protected areas

    17.4.1.1.5 Other

17.4.2 Cultural environment

For example, shipwrecks, IUCN natural world heritage sites etc.

17.4.3 Socio-economics

Identify adjacent coastal communities' regional demographic and economic issues that may arise within and outside of the project area, including whether this is a direct or indirect outcome of the physical, biological or socio-economic effects of the proposed development activity. (e.g. coastal resource use and exclusion zones). Include such aspects such as supply chain, utilities, access to water, fuel and impact to local communities in terms of access to supplies.

17.5 Summary of residual effects

18. Accidental events and natural hazards

Environmentally hazardous discharges resulting from accidental and extreme natural events are fundamentally different from normal operational discharges of wastes and waste waters. This section should outline the possibility/probability of accidental events occurring, the impact they may have, the measures taken to prevent or respond to such an event, and the residual impact should an event occur.

For each component include:

      A. *The nature and extent of any impact*

      B. *Measures that will be taken to avoid, mitigate or minimize such impact; and*

      C. *Residual impacts*

18.1 Extreme weather

18.2 Natural hazards

For example: volcanic eruption, seismic events, landslides, and soil erosion

18.3 Accidental events

For example: hazardous material leakage or spillage, fire and explosion, collisions, including potential loss of equipment.

19. Environmental management, monitoring and reporting

Sufficient information should be provided to enable the State to anticipate possible environmental management, monitoring and reporting requirements for an environmental permit. Information listed should reflect the proponent's environmental policy (Environment Management System) and the translation of that policy to meet the requirements under this section and previous sections during different stages in the project life, i.e. from construction to decommissioning and closure. Information detailed in this section should include, but not be limited to, the headings below:

19.1 Organizational structure and responsibilities

This section should show how the Contractor's environmental team fits into its overall organizational structure. Responsibilities of key personnel should be outlined.

19.2 Environmental Management System (EMS)

Although a full EMS may not exist at the time the EIA is submitted, this section should outline the standards that will be considered and/or aligned with in developing the EMS for the project.

19.3 Environmental Management Plan (EMP)

An EMP will be submitted as a separate document for the country's approval prior to exploitation operations commencing. This section should provide an overview of what an EMP would entail. This section shall include, as a minimum, the following headings:

19.3.1 Mitigation and Management

This section should summarize the actions and commitments that have arisen from the impact minimization and mitigation strategies. Differentiate rehabilitation strategies for during operations and those for closure.

19.3.2 Monitoring plan

This section should summarize the monitoring plan approach and programme.

19.3.2.1 Approach

19.3.2.2 Programme

This section should provide an overview of the envisaged monitoring programme (it is noted further detail will be provided in the EMP).

19.3.3 Closure plan

It is expected that a closure plan will be submitted as a separate document for the Regulatory Authority's approval. However, this section should provide an overview of what the closure plan will entail, including decommissioning, continued monitoring and rehabilitation measures, if applicable.

19.4 Reporting

19.4.1 Monitoring

This section should outline how results of monitoring studies will be reported to the Regulatory Authority.

19.4.2 Incident Reporting

This section should outline how incidents will be reported.

20. References

This section should provide details of reference materials used in sourcing information and/or data used in the EIA report.

21. Appendices

All supporting studies should be attached in Appendices. Include technical reports carried out for parts of EIA (e.g. the ERA, other important studies, such as sediment plume modelling, eco-toxicity research). The Terms of Reference for the EIA report and the study team's CV and qualifications should also be attached as an appendix.

Annex IV: Participants

Dr Adrian Flynn
Director
Fathom Pacific Pty Ltd
Australia

Dr Akira Tsune
Chief Geologist, Exploration Department
Deep Ocean Resources Development
Japan

Ms Alison Swaddling
Environment Advisory
Pacific Community
Fiji

Ms Ana Paula Linhares
Robert Makgill Barrister
New Zealand

Dr Andrew Birtchenough
Principal Marine Advisor
Lowestoft Laboratory
Centre for Environment, Fisheries and
Aquaculture Science (Cefas)
United Kingdom

Mrs Camillia Garae
Geologist
Geology and Mines Unit
Ministry of Lands and Natural Resources
Vanuatu

Dr Carina Costa de Oliveira
Professor, Faculty of Law
University of Brasilia
Brazil

Dr Charles Morgan
Principal
Moana Hohonu Consulting LLC
Hawaii

Dr Chengwei Ju
China Ocean Mineral Resources Research and
Development Association
China

Mr Chris Brown
Northwest University of Politics and Law
China

Mr Christopher Mann
Director
Campaign for Health Oceans
Pew Environment Group
The Pew Charitable Trusts
United States of America

Professor Cindy Van Dover
Nicholas School of the Environment
Duke University
United States of America

Dr Daniel O.B. Jones
National Oceanography Centre
University of Southampton
United Kingdom

Dr David Billett
National Oceanography Centre
University of Southampton
United Kingdom

Dr Dheny Raw
Executive Officer – Legal
Department of Foreign Affairs and Trade
Australia

Professor Donald K. Anton
Griffith University
Australia

Mr Duncan E.J. Currie
Adviser
Deep Sea Conservation Coalition
Netherlands

Dr Edwin Egede
Cardiff School of Law & Politics
Cardiff University
Wales, United Kingdom

Mr Gerald McCormack
Cook Islands Natural Heritage Trust
Cook Islands

Dr Gwénaëlle Le Gurun
Legal Officer
International Seabed Authority
Jamaica

Mr Hans-Peter Damian
Umweltbundesamt
Federal Environment Agency
Germany

Dr Harald Ginzky
Umweltbundesamt
Federal Environment Agency
Germany

Ms Holly Matley
Attorney-General's Departmebt
Australia

Dr James R. Hein
Senior Scientist
United States Geological Survey
United States

Mr Jeff Ardron
Adviser Ocean Governance
Commonwealth Secretariat
London, United Kingdom

Ms Jennifer Warren
Director Regulatory
United Kingdom Seabed Resources
United Kingdom

Dr John Feenan
Director Mining Asia Pacific
Royal IHC

Mr Jonathan Lowe
Vice President of Exploration
Tonga Offshore Mining Ltd
Tonga

Mr Joseph Bertrand Sa'a Penandjo
Chief of Service of Mining Research Projects
Monitoring Unit
Department of Geology
Ministry of Mines, Industry and Technological
Development
Cameroon

Mr Juan Pablo Paniego
Office of the Legal Adviser
Ministry of Foreign Affairs and Worship
Argentina

Dr Kaiser de Souza
Senior Geology and Mineral Information Expert
African Mineral Development Center
United Nations Economic Commission for Africa

Ms Karen Hauff
General Counsel
Tonga Offshore Mining Litd
Tonga

Mr Kris Van Nijen
General Manager
Global Sea Mineral Resources NV

Ms Kristina Gjerde
Adjunct Professor
Middlebury Institute for International Studies at
Monterey
California, United States of America

Ms Laura Lallier
University of Ghent
Department of Public International European
Law
Belgium

Dr Malcolm R. Clark
National Institute of Water and Atmospheric Research
New Zealand

Dr Neil Craik
Associate Professor and Director
School of Environment, Enterprise and Development
University of Waterloo

Mr Paul Lynch
Seabed Minerals Authority
Cook Islands

Professor Pei-Yuan Qian
Hong Kong University of Science and Technology
Hong Kong

Dr Philomène Verlaan
University of Hawaii and Advisory Committee on Protection of the Sea
United Kingdom

Dr Rahkyun E Kim
Griffith University
Australia

Dr Ralph Spickermann
Chief Engineer
United Kingdom Seabed Resources
United Kingdom

Mrs Rena Lee
Senior State Counsel
International Affairs Division
Attorney-General's Chambers
Singapore

Ms Renee Grogan
Sustainable Manager
Nautilus Minerals

Mr Rezah Badal
Director General
Department for Continental Shelf
Maritime Zones Administration & Exploitation
Prime Minister's Office

Mr Richard Johnson
Environmental Protection Authority
New Zealand

Mr Robert Heydon
Nauru Ocean Resources Inc
Nauru

Mr Robert Makgill
Robert Makgill Barristers
New Zealand

Professor Robin Warner
Australian National Centre for Ocean Resources and Security
University of Wollongong
New South Wales
Australia

Professor Rosemary Rayfuse
Faculty of Law
University of New South Wales
Australia

Dr Russell Howorth
Member
Legal & Technical Commission
International Seabed Authority
Jamaica

Dr Sabine Christiansen
Institute for Advanced Sustainability Studies
Potsdam
Germany

Mr Sébastien Ybert
Institute français de recherché pour l'exploitation de la mer
France

Professor Shaojun Liu
China Ocean Mineral Resources Research and Development Association
China

Dr Simon Walmsley
Marine Manager
WWF International
Switzerland

Mr Takaaki Matsui
Japan Oil, Gas and Metals Corporation
Japan

Mr Tom De Wachter
Environmental Coordinator A
G-Tech Sea Mineral Resources NV
Belgium

Dr Tomohiko Fukushima
Deep Ocean Resources Development
Japan

Dr Tor Jensen
Vice President
DNV GL
Norway

Dr Ulrich Schwarz-Schampera
Federal Institute for Geosciences and Natural
Resources
Germany

Ms Xiangxin Xu
China Ocean Mineral Resources Research and
Development Association
China